M000009338

Weinstock's

SACRAMENTO'S FINEST DEPARTMENT STORE

Annette Kassis

Charleston · London

THE
History
PRESS

Published by The History Press
Charleston, SC 29403
www.historypress.net

Copyright © 2012 by Annette Kassis
All rights reserved

Images are courtesy of the Center for Sacramento History, Weinstock, Lubin Collection, unless otherwise noted.

First published 2012

Manufactured in the United States

ISBN 978.1.60949.444.5

Library of Congress CIP data applied for.

Notice: The information in this book is true and complete to the best of our knowledge. It is offered without guarantee on the part of the author or The History Press. The author and The History Press disclaim all liability in connection with the use of this book.

All rights reserved. No part of this book may be reproduced or transmitted in any form whatsoever without prior written permission from the publisher except in the case of brief quotations embodied in critical articles and reviews.

For Rich…for always

CONTENTS

CONTENTS

ACKNOWLEDGEMENTS

No one undertakes an endeavor like this alone. I have incurred many debts in the course of completing this book, and it gives me a great deal of pleasure to publicly thank those who have helped me.

I am particularly indebted to the Center for Sacramento History. This was not my first research project at the archive, and it certainly will not be my last. City historian Marcia Eymann put me in touch with The History Press and got this ball rolling. Archivist Patricia Johnson and deputy city historian Dylan McDonald were instrumental in leading me through the wonderful Weinstock-Lubin Collection and sending me in directions I might otherwise not have gone. Photographs archivist Rebecca Crowther plowed through mountains of images with me and helped me select the seventy images that made it into the final version of this book. The extra TLC she gave the images during the scanning process is much appreciated.

There is, perhaps, no greater test of friendship than editing a friend's manuscript, but three very special people undertook the daunting task, and their efforts have made me a better writer. Historian Michael Adamson put aside work on his own book to read mine, and he provided a more thorough and in-depth critique and analysis than I had the right to expect. My best friend and former business partner Roma Heerhartz employed the same editing skills and attention to detail that she used when editing my work throughout the twenty years we owned our advertising agency. My sister, Frances Rae, brought her own editing skills to the project as she went through my manuscript, not once, but twice. I am also indebted to her for digging up information about Louisa Lyons Lubin's whereabouts after she left Sacramento in 1896. I look forward to returning the favor and editing Fran's work soon.

My mother, Gertrude Stout, has been an enthusiastic supporter of this project from the beginning. Her encouragement was enormously helpful, and it was her comments that I kept uppermost in my mind as I selected the images for this book.

When there is a book project in the house, the entire family lives with it, like it or not. My own family has been tremendously supportive and, lucky for me, genuinely interested. My son, Michael, has always believed in and encouraged me—a wonderful trait he inherited from his father. My husband, Rich, has been my chief source of support throughout the research and writing process. He was promoting this book to anyone and everyone before I had even completed the first draft, and he cleared the path in a thousand different ways so that I had the time to write. Even when I was at my most stressed, he never lost that all-important and ever-present marvelous sense of humor. I could not have done this without him.

INTRODUCTION

When I first mentioned to family, friends and acquaintances that I was writing a history of Weinstock's, I invariably heard responses along the lines of: "I remember Weinstock's! I loved shopping there. Whatever happened to them?" For longtime residents of Sacramento, Weinstock's—or Weinstock, Lubin—had always been here. What very few knew was how Weinstock's came to be, and most did not realize the department store was a homegrown business with its roots deep in post–gold rush Sacramento. Further, I found that for some, the name Lubin had disappeared entirely from memories of the store, and others were not aware that Weinstock's had ever been Weinstock, Lubin. David Lubin, who began the store and was both instrumental to its success and a leader in establishing its progressive policies toward employees and customers, moved on to undertake a personal mission to improve economic conditions for farmers and provide stability to the world's food supply. His contributions beyond Sacramento's business landscape should not be forgotten, so I have included parts of David Lubin's story beyond Weinstock's in this book as well.

In addition to being "Sacramento's Finest Department Store," Weinstock, Lubin was also an innovator, although "innovative" may seem an odd way to describe the Sacramento business. Most historians of American department stores and consumer culture focus their attention on the major population centers of the Northeast and Midwest, and for good reason. The development of the department store out of the nineteenth-century dry goods store was concentrated in those regions. The West—particularly the far West—was farther from the centers of industry, bourgeois culture and fashion. For that same reason, however, business development in the West, particularly in California, bears more direct study. Without the established distribution and manufacturing networks of more developed parts of the country to rely on, some independent business owners developed their own methods and creative solutions to new problems and—as in the case of David Lubin—adopted new ideas early on that were just beginning to take hold on the other side of the country.

The innovations David Lubin and his half brother, Harris Weinstock, brought to Sacramento included the "one-price" concept, by which merchandise was sold for the price clearly marked; new design for overalls; the eight-hour workday; employee profit sharing; and a company-owned vacation retreat for employees and their families. Outside the business, David Lubin changed how farmers received market information on a global scale. His International Institute of Agriculture (IIA), established in Rome in 1906, eventually became the present-day United Nations Food and Agriculture Organization.

The innovative spirit of Weinstock's did not end with David Lubin and Harris Weinstock. Indeed, after World War II, the company was only the second department store in the United States to have a woman as its president. Throughout the company's existence—even as it became part of one of the largest retail chains in the country—Weinstock's maintained its community feel, local management roots and willingness to innovate. As you will see later in the narrative, Weinstock's employees were also at the leading edge of computer usage in retail. Unfortunately, innovation in employee relations, customer service and technology were not enough to save Weinstock's and its parent company, Carter Hawley Hale, from a series of hostile takeover bids followed by a major economic downturn. That, too, is part of Weinstock's and its history.

The story of Weinstock, Lubin & Co. is told here through archival and manuscript collections, biographies, oral histories, newspapers and periodicals and interviews and commentary from former employees. I have also referenced the works of other historians of department stores and consumer culture. Their research provided the necessary context in which to place the Weinstock's story. Any errors, however, are entirely my own.

Weinstock's was distinctly Sacramento; it was ours. If the following pages touch on your memories, I hope I did those memories justice.

D. Lubin, One Price, 1874–1891

I set out to find a place to start in, but nothing suitable offered in San Francisco, so I resolved to go up the river to Sacramento and see what chances there were in the State capital.
—*David Lubin*

David Lubin's first store expansion began with his arrest.

One night, as he attempted to sleep under the counter of his tiny dry goods establishment, he grew increasingly frustrated with the noise coming from the Chinese laundry next door. A fan-tan game was in progress, as it was on most nights. As the game became more raucous, Lubin became increasingly angry. Finally reaching the end of his patience, he smashed through the flimsy partition between his dry goods store and the laundry. There are various accounts of exactly what damage was done that night, ranging from crashing through the wall and breaking up the game to physical altercation with the gamblers. In his own words, Lubin admits to smashing a mirror on his side of the wall and breaking through a panel in the partition separating the two business concerns. The end result was a summons for David Lubin to appear in court.

"I don't know how many charges they had against me; house-breaking, assault and battery and what not," he mused. When the judge asked Lubin what he had to say, Lubin related his story and told the judge about the noisy fan-tan game and his efforts to stop it. Attempts to crack down on gambling and frequent raids on fan-tan parlors were commonplace during this time, and upon hearing that gambling was at the root of the disturbance, the judge dismissed the charges against Lubin but "fined the Chinamen fifty or sixty dollars for gambling." This, however, was not the end of the story. Later that day, the landlord showed up at Lubin's business and accused him of robbing him of his tenants. The Chinese tenants resolved to move after the incident and had given notice to the landlord. When the landlord told Lubin what he had been getting for the space, Lubin said, "I will give you that for the room." The partition was knocked down, and overnight the store was enlarged to double its size.[1]

Most business histories do not begin with movie-worthy fight scenes and illegal gambling parlors. The inception of Weinstock's, however, was rooted in David Lubin's perception of the American West. The time he spent as a gold miner in Arizona had left the young man with a stubborn streak and a direct and plain-speaking manner that would be hallmarks of his character for the rest of his life. It is no wonder that this intense and frank man attempted to deal directly and abruptly with a problem—"frontier style," he would say—and wound up in front of a judge. David Lubin was never shy about speaking his mind.

THE SHTETL-BORN COWBOY

Lubin did not look like the dime novel's image of a cowboy. Indeed, his roots in a small Jewish community in Russian-controlled Poland were as far removed from the popular idea of a cowboy as one could get. Born in 1849 at Klodawa, near Cracow, Lubin was "marked for greatness" at an early age. Family lore has it that, four days after his birth, the burning wick from a Sabbath candle blew off and dropped on the baby's cheek, leaving a scar that would remain for life. A rabbi visiting from the synagogue pointed out to the distressed parents that this mark from the Sabbath candle indicated that the child was chosen by the Lord for his service. Because of the rabbi's words, so the story goes, Lubin was named for the king of Israel, David, rather than Pinchus, after his grandfather, as was custom. Although David Lubin himself did not believe in omens, he acknowledged that his mother's belief in the sign and how that belief influenced the manner in which he was reared had "given a turn to his whole life."[2]

While he was still an infant, Lubin's father died in a cholera epidemic. His mother, Rachel, married Solomon Weinstock. Shortly thereafter, life for the Jews in Russian Poland became intolerable. Following a pogrom during which Rachel hid in a cellar with her children, the family fled to London. There they remained for about two years. Harris Weinstock, David Lubin's half brother and future business partner, was born in London in 1854. In 1855, when Lubin was not quite six years old, the entire family sailed for New York.[3]

Growing up in New York, Lubin exhibited both a strong sense of adventure and a deep love of learning. His brother Harris recalled that Lubin's studious habits and "hunger for knowledge" were contagious and provided an example for the younger sibling. In 1861, shortly after the start of the Civil War, poverty necessitated that Lubin begin working at about the age of twelve and halt his formal education.[4]

He followed his older brother, Simon, to Massachusetts, where David began working for a jeweler and goldsmith and lived under Simon's watchful eye. David earned $3.60 per week, which he gave to Simon for room and board, but Simon soon tired of being responsible for the youth. He sent David off to find a job elsewhere, expecting the boy to earn enough to pay room and board on his own. David went four miles up the road to North Attleboro, Massachusetts, where he found a job soldering and polishing for the Morse Brothers. After a bit of a rocky start, Lubin quickly settled into the job and spent the remainder of the Civil War manufacturing military items, such as the blue goggles used by General William T. Sherman's troops in their march through Georgia, and developing a natural aptitude for invention and manufacture. In an effort to get his work done quickly so he could go play, the young boy developed a method by which he could solder a dozen goggles at once rather than one at a time as he had been taught to do by his boss. Lubin's method was perfected and adopted by his employers, but he received no financial compensation for it.[5]

HEADING WEST, THE FIRST TIME

When the Civil War ended, David Lubin headed for the Pacific Coast. His older and much-beloved sister Jeannette's marriage and move to California with her husband provided the impetus for his own journey westward. Lubin's biographer and friend, Olivia Rossetti Agresti, noted that no record remained of Lubin's trek across the continent but that in his later years he told her of time spent working as a jeweler in San Francisco before he headed south to Los Angeles, a village at the time. Described by Agresti as being strong and fond of manly sports, Lubin seemed to enjoy the pioneering life, and in

1868, at the age of nineteen, after working for a few months in a Los Angeles lumberyard, he joined up with a group headed to Arizona in search of gold.

In fact, Lubin's time in Arizona does read something like a dime novel. A collection of adventure and profit seekers under the leadership of a man identified only as Captain Kirby hit the trail for Arizona with a pack of horses and mules and not much else. At some point on the trek, Lubin and his horse became separated from the group and wandered in the desert for almost two days. Allowing his exhausted horse to go its own way rather than attempt to guide it, Lubin was saved only by stumbling upon his own party again toward the end of the second day. The group had almost given up hope of finding him. The incident left a deep impression on him. Many years later, he wrote to the governor of Arizona, "It is perhaps not without reason that the great religious prophets, the Moses, the Elijahs, the Johns and the Mohammeds, obtained their inspiration from the desert."[6]

By virtue of her religion, Rachel Lubin Weinstock taught her children that to insult or attack someone because of the color of his skin was to rebuke God. Her lessons, however, did not prevent attacks by others. Racial and ethnic tensions directed at Native Americans and at Lubin himself exploded on this expedition, and these also, according to Agresti, made a significant impact on the young man and how he would later do business. In one instance, a man in the group overheard Lubin singing old Hebrew songs to himself as he worked. The man asked him what he was singing, and Lubin explained that they were songs he had learned as a child. When pressed as to what language it was, Lubin informed the man that it was Hebrew. The man accused Lubin of being a "damned Jew," and a fight broke out. The bigot got the worst of it, and when word of the incident made it to Kirby, he was sent on his way.[7]

Following his Arizona adventure, Lubin returned to New York by way of Chicago, carrying little with him, as the Arizona excursion had not proved a profitable one. While in New York, he took a job with a lamp-manufacturing firm and sold its products on the road. Living with his mother and her sister, Lubin's aunt recalled that he would return from these selling trips armed with new books, new ideas and new foods. Lubin was, as his aunt Fanny Bonnheim noted, a "moody, erratic, hot-tempered youth." The younger children were in awe of him—not least, one would imagine, because of his Arizona "cowboy" adventures—and they were often admonished to be quiet and not disturb David while he was engrossed in his books. Upon returning to New York from one of these selling trips, a coal-oil lamp exploded and almost burned down his mother's home. Subsequently, Lubin invented a non-explosive coal-

Half brothers David Lubin (left) and Harris Weinstock, circa 1875. *Courtesy of the Center for Sacramento History, Sacramento Ethnic Survey Collection, and the Judah Magnes Museum.*

oil lamp patented by his employers and sold at a sizeable profit. It was the second of many inventions that would come from Lubin, and the second to be patented by his employer rather than by himself. Still, the financial windfall to Lubin was enough to send him on his first trip to Europe.

When he returned to New York, he learned that his sister Jeannette had recently been widowed and had come into a small sum of money, which she used to open a dry goods store in San Francisco. She had already sent for young Harris Weinstock to come out and help, and now she invited David to join them and invest his savings in the business. He agreed, and in 1874, at age twenty-four or twenty-five, he made the trip back to California and rejoined this segment of his family in San Francisco.[8]

RETURN TO CALIFORNIA

This time around, the intent behind Lubin's travels was settling down, not looking for adventure. Working with Harris in San Francisco, David learned how business was conducted. During this era, it was customary that prices were not fixed; the merchant asked for a sum, and the customer would haggle with the merchant until a price was agreed upon. The system of bargaining and haggling was particularly hateful to Lubin. By his own admission, he could not rationalize the process, and it made him a poor businessman. As he told Olivia Agresti many years later, one incident in particular provided the idea for a new store in a new place with a new method of doing business. Lubin was alone in the San Francisco store when a sailor came in, and he decided to see what kind of salesman he could really be. He proceeded to do quite a bit of business with the man, taking almost thirty dollars from him for goods not worth nearly that much. "But when the transaction was over," Lubin told Agresti, "I had made up my mind. It was wrong. I would have nothing more to do with it, and I determined that I would start for myself on the basis of fixed prices on all goods, marked in plain figures so that all could read."[9]

When David Lubin sought to open his new dry goods emporium in Sacramento, he was charting new territory. Arriving in Sacramento in 1874, Lubin selected a ten- by twelve-foot space on a corner of K Street and set up shop. The little store sat above a basement saloon, across from saloons on two other corners, and shared a thin partition with the aforementioned neighboring Chinese laundry that would later become the catalyst for the store's first expansion. Lubin settled into the space, made shelves, set up a counter made from dry goods boxes covered with an oil cloth and hung out his sign: D. Lubin, One Price. "I used to get my meals for 'two bits' on the floor above me where there was a boarding place, and a sloppy place it was too. I rigged up a bunk in the store, under the counter, and slept there," he recalled. The setup was rugged, and the stock was minimal. Lubin sold clothing, primarily to workers at the Central Pacific Railroad, and other dry goods staples such as collar buttons, pocketknives and handkerchiefs. David Lubin did not invent the one-price concept, but fixed pricing was relatively rare before 1880 and certainly not well known or understood west of the Mississippi River. Fixed prices began to become the norm between 1880 and 1915, when more manufactured and ready-to-wear merchandise was sold by merchants and when generic food items sold in bulk began to be sold prepackaged and under brand names.[10]

His one-price policy was not well received by the locals. When customers insisted on haggling, Lubin stood firm that they pay the price marked or leave his store with nothing. Many did, in fact, leave with nothing, and Lubin, by his own admission, sometimes lacked the twenty-five cents per meal charged by the upstairs boardinghouse.[11]

One of David Lubin's first big financial breaks is a story that became local legend, as it was repeated in Weinstock, Lubin anniversary publications and employee newsletters and recounted in newspapers.

As Lubin tells it, a "great big chap" came into the store and proceeded to select about twenty-five dollars worth of merchandise, the largest single piece of business in the early days of the store. As Lubin was wrapping the goods, the customer noticed a pocketknife, priced at fifty cents, in a small display case. The customer asked that Lubin throw in the pocketknife with his other purchases. Lubin explained that he could not do that as it was against the principle of the store. "If I gave him a knife I should presently have to give presents to other people, and…such a course would be inconsistent with an equitable mode of doing business," Lubin recounted. The customer insisted, noting that he had not tried to "beat down" Lubin on any of the other goods. When Lubin still refused, the customer told him he could keep his "damned traps." Lubin threw the parcels on a shelf and told the customer he would "not sell them to him anyhow, that he could just get out and go to hell."

The customer was sent on his way, but while Lubin was at lunch a different man came to the store and bought the parcels on the shelf from the young boy who minded the shop while Lubin was out. "He bought them for himself, but they went to that big chap, all right," Lubin noted. The following Saturday night, as he was getting ready to close for the evening, Lubin heard a loud rumble on the board sidewalk. It was a crowd headed straight for his store. Fearing a fight, Lubin was stunned when instead he heard the leader of the group—the customer he had turned away a few days earlier—shout, "There he is! He's the only honest storekeeper in Sacramento, boys. Whatever he says is so. Let's buy him out!" The group proceeded to buy Lubin out of almost everything in stock—at the fixed price of each item. As it turned out, the customer in Lubin's story of the argument and eventual buy-out was the foreman of the boiler shops at the Central Pacific Railroad Company works. When the story of the foreman and the one-price store got out, business began to turn around for David Lubin.[12]

Almost overnight, the store began to burst out of its ten-by-twelve space. Perhaps recent business success coupled with the inability to enlarge the store space contributed to Lubin's angry eruption directed at the fan-tan gamblers next door. It is at this point that Lubin smashed through the wall, got arrested and then ultimately rented that additional area from the landlord. With capital presumably provided thanks to the dramatic increase in business, Lubin was able to undertake the much-needed expansion and begin to add staff.

Another early break came through the first of many inventions patented by Lubin himself: the "endless-fly overall." Lubin's overalls were designed with an innovation that prevented them from splitting open at the crotch, a common problem with other overalls according to the railroad workers who complained to him about inferior products. Lubin's overalls sold for seventy-five cents a pair, half the price of the riveted overalls that were nearest in quality to the endless-fly design. An active publicity campaign ensured that the overalls took the lead in the local market. They were in great demand by the mechanics from the nearby Central Pacific Railroad boiler shops, and Lubin manufactured them in Sacramento.[13] The one-price dry goods store was growing closer to diversifying into one of California's earliest department stores.

FROM ONE PRICE TO THE MECHANICS' STORE

It is unclear exactly when Harris closed the San Francisco dry goods emporium and joined his half brother in Sacramento, but by 1875 both men were working in the Sacramento shop, and the business had a new name: the Mechanics' Store.

The Mechanics' Store consistently advertised beginning in 1875. The large newspaper ads written by David Lubin were long on preachy copy and short on merchandise details. The overarching idea was that the Mechanics' Store was the place to shop because you would be treated fairly and honestly, and the merchandise would not be misrepresented in terms of quality and source. Because brand names were not yet pervasive, there was really no

David Lubin's one-price store became the Mechanics' Store sometime after Harris Weinstock's arrival in Sacramento. Circa 1878.

need to specify particular items in the ads. The customer only needed to know that the Mechanics' Store carried items traditionally found in a dry goods emporium and that the prices were set, plainly marked and fair. David Lubin was not the only merchant to write less-than-stellar advertising copy. A 1909 advertising copywriting manual noted that dry goods advertisements contained some of the worst writing in the industry, since store owners like Lubin often felt they were the best people to write these "folksy" ads.[14]

Lubin's early ads were targeted primarily at the dishonesty of his competition, referred to as "grabbers," by focusing on their greed and comparing them to tyrannical tax collectors with headlines like: "'Ah! Give me back the days of '49!' cried a grabber, 'Those were the days when times were flush!'"; "We will not submit to Unjust Taxation"; and "Workmen, Read & Think!"

In a bold move, Lubin even challenged the California legislature to be more like the Mechanics' Store in its dealings:

Gentlemen of the Senate & of the Assembly!
Now is Your Time to Make a Record!
We want you to be HONEST; if you are so, then we want you to remain so.
We want you to serve Sacramento, and not your party.
Do not sell your vote, but work hard for the interest and benefit of those
who elected you, and create a GOOD RECORD, and Sacramento is able and
willing to reward you for the same. Take example from the proprietors of
THE MECHANICS' STORE
Who, a little over three years ago, started a store here on a very small
scale, hardly as large as their private office is now, and with a capital of
a few hundred dollars, and by hard work, perseverance, energy, enterprise
and determination, have created, out of almost nothing,
The Largest Retail House on the Pacific Coast

By 1877, David Lubin and Harris Weinstock employed forty-three people and could claim to be the leading merchant in Sacramento, boasting not only the lowest prices on the Pacific Coast but also complete stock in ten or more lines, including clothing, boots and shoes, trunks, valises and satchels, blankets, quilts and comforters and cutlery and jewelry.[15]

Like other family-operated dry goods stores of the period, the Mechanics' Store responded to the changing economic needs of the growing Sacramento economy by evolving into a department store. Marketing practices and management techniques became more like those employed by the large department stores such as John Wanamaker in Philadelphia, Marshall

The Mechanics' Store gradually enlarged, adding new items along with the additional square footage. Circa 1880.

Field in Chicago and R.H. Macy in New York. As the Mechanics' Store grew and began carrying a greater variety of mass-produced merchandise, customers began to buy more mass-produced goods, developing a firmly established consumer society in the Sacramento region. Changes across the country, from diversification of merchandise and use of the one-price system to allowing free customer access to stores without obligation to buy, were moving retailing into a new era.[16]

By 1881, Lubin and Weinstock, still operating under the name the Mechanics' Store, were able to boast several separate departments: Dry Goods, Fancy Goods, Men's Furnishing Goods, Men's Clothing, Boys' Clothing, Ladies' Suit and Cloak Department, Yankee Notions, Hats and Caps, Millinery, Boots and Shoes, Wholesale Department, Country Order Department, Manufacturing Department and a mail-order business. Some of the departments bear further explanation, as they are not typical of what department stores later became. The "Yankee Notions" department included items such as soap, stationery, brushes, combs, pocketknives, purses, perfume and other items that a Yankee peddler would likely have carried on the road. "Fancy Goods" were items like gloves, hosiery, corsets, laces, jewelry, ribbons, cuffs and other "articles of personal adornment." The "Country Order" Department was, simply, a fulfillment unit. The department filled between one hundred and two hundred orders daily, with the goods sent primarily by mail. "Selectors" acting on behalf of the customer pulled the desired items under the mandate that they exercise the "fairest and best judgment in behalf of the intending buyer."[17]

Ladies' clothing was not ready-to-wear. Clothing for women was ordered based on illustrations in the catalogue, with style and finish details determining price. Lubin and Weinstock assured their customers that ordering from them meant they would receive a garment "designed and made in accordance with the newest fashions, and that the cost was far lower than if the same garment were made at home or purchased elsewhere "ready-made." The catalogue also noted that new styles were being continually added as the season progressed. If the customer did not find anything suitable in the catalogue, a garment could be made-to-order so long as proper measurements were sent along with the age of the wearer, a description of the desired style and a dollar amount to be spent. Most American stores would not contain departments with a full range of women's ready-to-wear styles until around 1915.[18]

During the 1870s and 1880s, very few dry goods emporia had transformed themselves into full-fledged department stores. By the 1880s, only exceptional stores like R.H. Macy & Company in New York and Marshall Field & Company in Chicago carried household goods and other items beyond the typical dry goods emporium stock. But as department stores expanded, one historian notes, they revealed the scope of what the American economy was producing and importing.[19]

With the 1880 publication of a "modest pamphlet," as they called it, David Lubin and Harris Weinstock expanded their business with mail order, setting themselves far apart from their competitors and entering a new arena in marketing. The publication of their 1881 catalogue predated the mail-order catalogue of Sears, Roebuck and Co. by several years and came just a few years after the appearance of the Montgomery Ward catalogue. By 1891, Weinstock, Lubin & Co. could boast the largest mail-order business on the West Coast and tout an annual catalogue reach of 250,000 readers.[20]

WEINSTOCK, LUBIN & CO.

With articles of incorporation filed on January 10, 1888, David Lubin and Harris Weinstock established themselves as Weinstock, Lubin & Co., a name that would hold until the 1960s. David Lubin was listed as president and Harris Weinstock as vice-president, but the younger brother's name was listed first in the company because, Lubin reasoned, Harris would do a better job if his name came first. The new name, in the style of the large department stores back east, was indicative of the new status of the Sacramento business. Minutes from early board of directors meetings show just how much the business had grown and how forward-thinking and innovative Weinstock and Lubin were, especially as employers. Between

1888 and 1890, the board agreed to continue the system of profit sharing for heads of departments and employees that had been established in 1883. In addition, it discussed sick leave benefits, elocution lessons for employees and a program of educating lower-level employees so they could be promoted to assistant buyer positions.[21]

It had become obvious by this time that the store had to expand. Rather than build on a new site, however, Weinstock, Lubin & Co. expanded the way many department stores of that period did: by erecting a new building around the existing one. The old Mechanics' Store had grown in size over time as additions were tacked onto the existing structure and connected to the main store via a series of bridges. As departments were added and the name was changed to Weinstock, Lubin & Co., it became increasingly apparent that a new building was sorely needed. Weinstock and Lubin wanted the new store in the same location as the old, and they did not want to interrupt business to build it. The outside walls were built around the existing store, with business conducted as usual. As interior spaces were readied, departments were transferred into them. The construction was said to be "one of the most interesting feats ever witnessed in Sacramento."[22]

As the store, now Weinstock, Lubin & Co., continued to expand, a new building was constructed around the existing structure. Business continued as usual during construction, and stock was moved from department to department as each new section of the building was completed. Circa 1890.

In 1891, a new Weinstock, Lubin & Co. store began to take shape as the three-story building was constructed around the 400–12 K Street location. An illustration of the new store graced the back cover of the spring and summer 1891 catalogue. Running 140 feet along K Street and 160 feet along Fourth Street, the building was designed with three rows of galleries on all sides and display windows set back ten feet from the sidewalk to create an arcade between the large display windows and the sidewalk. When the new store opened in November, the *Sacramento Daily Bee* pronounced it "striking and attractive," stating, "The most noticeable feature of the architectural design is the arcade front, with massive plate glass windows as a background. The entire front of the lower story is a series of magnificent show windows." The building's architect was W.H. Hamilton of Sacramento, and the general contractors were Sprague & Elliott, also a local company. Sacramentan Adolph Teichert laid the artificial stone pavement along the K Street sidewalk and under the arcade. There was no grand opening. A front-page ad in the November 24, 1891 edition of the *Daily Bee* said simply, "The New Store Ready for Business. Too Busy for Formal Opening. Weinstock, Lubin & Co."[23]

The Big White Store at the corner of Fourth and K Streets, circa 1900.

DEPARTMENT STORES: A NEW KIND OF STORE

Post–Civil War market demands, manufacturing methods and more efficient systems of distribution played key roles in the creation of department stores. As the American economy moved toward a commodity exchange market and away from an economy based more heavily on barter, department stores became palatial showplaces for goods. The desirable was on full display as department store windows showcased fashion and fantasy in a way never before seen by the average, none-too-well-traveled American citizen. The vast array of items on display changed the way people viewed both the goods and themselves. Department stores were as much about the psychological space they occupied in the public's imagination as the physical space they occupied in a city.[24]

The show windows of the beautiful new Weinstock, Lubin & Co. that opened its doors on November 24, 1891, represented the very latest in merchandise display. Prior to the mid-1880s, show windows in the modern sense were almost nonexistent, and many stores put nothing at all in their windows, considering the idea of displaying goods in such a way tasteless.

The Men's Department in the Big White Store, circa 1902.

There was also a lack of understanding in terms of how to go about displaying goods. In 1889, just two years before the opening of the new, modern Weinstock, Lubin & Co. store, the merchandising publication *Dry Goods Economist* changed its editorial focus from finance to retailing, encouraging merchants to "show your goods." By the late nineteenth century, department stores such as Weinstock, Lubin had joined churches, the media and other civic institutions as authorities on the American standard of living. More people were moving from farms to urban centers, America was now home to millions of immigrants and the United States was beginning to take its place as a power on the world stage. Department stores and their mind-boggling display windows showed foreign visitors, citizens and immigrants alike that America "had the goods" and could provide the ingredients of the good life. Department stores were more than happy to display just how all these new goods could be used to enhance living as the country and its citizens neared the start of the twentieth century.[25]

Stores began decorating their windows sometime around 1890, when the new Weinstock, Lubin building was in the planning stages. Early window displays focused more on displaying massive quantities of merchandise rather than presenting artistic displays designed to convey an image or idea along with the products displayed. L. Frank Baum, best known as the author of the children's classic *The Wonderful Wizard of Oz*, was a pioneer in theatrical window display, which he viewed as a form of advertising necessary to give store merchandise more "drawing power." By 1898, Baum had founded the National Association of Window Trimmers and published the first issue of the trade magazine the *Show Window*. Thanks to designers like Baum, merchants were beginning to understand the importance of how their windows were used and how critical a professional approach was to the value of the display. At roughly the same time, customers of all social classes were beginning to demand style in clothing and household goods. Artistic display windows helped establish a store's reputation as chic and up-to-date. Rather than trading in the basics as dry goods emporia had done, department stores sold fashion, style, middle-class living and the components necessary to achieve that lifestyle.[26]

Indeed, this emphasis on display and the meaning of goods as a vehicle to achieving a desired middle-class lifestyle appears to be precisely the intent behind the new Weinstock, Lubin store design. The arcade front and its promenade along the "massive plate glass windows" of the new store were described by one reporter as the "most noticeable feature of the architectural design." Built over and around the current Weinstock, Lubin location, the

Customers were seated at the counter as salespeople waited on them, circa 1902.

interior was, nonetheless, vastly different from the structure it was replacing. The store was not simply three floors stacked one atop the other. Floors two and three were spacious galleries and balconies that projected from the four sides of the interior, leaving the center of the building open with a height of fifty-seven feet from floor to ceiling at the central point of the building's distinctive arch. The glass alone in the new building was reported to cost about $5,000 (roughly $122,000 in 2011 dollars).

The windows were functional as well as beautiful. Although Weinstock, Lubin and the *Sacramento Union* had cosponsored a steam generator–driven display of electric lights during State Fair week in 1879, Sacramento did not have a consistent source of electrical power until 1895. Natural light was better than gas light for seeing the true color and detail of the merchandise, and shoppers frequently asked to take merchandise over to a window so they could make a better determination as to desirability. But the most unique feature of the new store, according to the *Daily Bee*, was the system of six bridges radiating from the center of the building to the first gallery. The bridges were twenty feet above the main floor, and along the center of each bridge was a double row of shelving. The amount of shelving on the bridges

Weinstock, Lubin employees Lottie Ready (left) and Margaret Miller (right), circa 1895.

was so immense, the newspaper reported, that if laid in a straight line, it would reach almost two and a half times the length of the K Street block on which the store sat.[27]

The opening of the store was an event the likes of which had never been seen in Sacramento. The big display window in front of the store was beautifully decorated for the occasion. Crowds gathered to look; suddenly, the floor of the display window opened, and a huge pink rose came up through the floor. Slowly, the petals of the rose unfolded, and a young Pearl Labhard—dressed as a small fairy bearing a star-tipped wand—stepped out of the rose and flitted about the window display trying on hats and incorporating the merchandise into her little show. After twenty minutes, she stepped back into the rose, the petals slowly closed and the flower disappeared back under the floor. Sacramento crowds lined the sidewalk outside the store and pressed against the glass just to catch a glimpse of this show, which occurred three times a day for one week.[28] The store was stunning, and although the name on the building was Weinstock, Lubin & Co., because of its color, locals took to referring to it as the "Big White Store."

The beautiful building would last only eleven years.

II
THE BIG WHITE STORE, 1891-1904

We propose to take off our coats and go to work with more energy than ever.
—Harris Weinstock

E ven before the beautiful 1891 department store opened, David Lubin
had removed himself from day-to-day operations to begin the work
that would be his most lasting legacy. By 1884, the brothers were successful
enough that David could fulfill a long-standing promise and take his mother,
Rachel, on a trip to Palestine. The trip and his exposure to the farmers of
the region proved to be life-changing. Upon his return home, he began to
focus on agriculture.[1]

Ever the inventor, Lubin held a number of patents on new and useful
improvements in agricultural machines, including the Lubin clod crusher
and cultivator, patented in 1887. He championed farmer collectives and
worked toward making it possible for the small grower to be treated fairly
in the marketplace, rather than to be "sold out" by middlemen. As the main
promoters of the California Fruit Exchange, Lubin and Weinstock lobbied to
get railroads to hook refrigerated cars to their trains. This was the beginning of
California's growth as a powerful agricultural state. The refrigerated railroad
cars carried the produce to the Midwest, and as California's produce trade
began to prosper, so did that of Washington and Oregon. This success would
provide the springboard for Lubin's later agricultural work—work that would
be on an international scale and would make David Lubin a prominent,
sometimes troubling, figure among legislators, presidents and kings.[2]

PULVERIZING THE SOIL WITH THE LUBIN PULVERIZER AND CLOD CRUSHER.

Advertisement for the Lubin clod crusher, patented by David Lubin in 1887. Lubin held at least nine patents.

By this time, David Lubin and Harris Weinstock were well-known, prominent men in Sacramento, with wives, children and standing in the community. In addition to being among the city's premier merchants, the half brothers were deeply involved in community affairs, as well. It was David Lubin who in 1885 presented the idea to Margaret Crocker of turning her home and private art collection over to the City of Sacramento as the Crocker Art Museum, the first public art museum founded in the western United States. Weinstock, who was active in the organization of the state militia, served in the California National Guard from 1881 to 1895, preferring from that point onward to be called "Colonel." In 1891, Harris Weinstock was elected one of fifteen freeholders by the City of Sacramento to begin the arduous process of writing a new city charter to replace the long since inadequate charter of 1863. In addition to Harris, the charter committee included future mayor Clinton White and attorney/ legislator Grove L. Johnson. The new charter was completed in March 1892 and formally adopted in 1893. By the time of the new charter's adoption, Lubin's interest in agriculture and the economic plight of the small farmer had led him into a tariff fight that would absorb him completely, even to the destruction of his marriage.[3]

This page: Harris Weinstock (top), circa 1900, and David Lubin (left), circa 1913. The painting of David Lubin from which this photograph was taken hangs in the offices of the Food and Agriculture Organization (FAO) of the United Nations in Rome, Italy.

Differing Personalities

Harris Weinstock and David Lubin—whom Harris called "Dave"—shared a sense of how their business should be run and how employees and customers were to be treated, but from that commonality their personalities diverged sharply. It was said that where Lubin could sometimes rub other businesspeople the wrong way due largely to his intense belief that life should be lived simply and wealth should not be accumulated, Harris was something of a ladies' man, a charmer and a man possessed of a wonderful sense of humor. As business prospered, he enjoyed his money, his family and his friends. While a full six inches shorter than six-foot-tall Harris, David had the more formidable appearance. By contrast, Harris enjoyed his

Harris Weinstock, seen here about to step down from a carriage, was regarded by many as more outgoing than his half brother.

wealth, living well and entertaining often, and on many occasions he paid all expenses to bring lecturers and seminars to his synagogue in Sacramento. He called his wife, Barbara, "Bob" (it is said he had nicknames for almost everyone), maintained a seemingly happy marriage and ran a highly prosperous, influential business.[4]

Weinstock, Lubin & Co. was the preeminent department store in Sacramento. Innovations instituted from the outset of the business now translated into a department store considered modern and leading edge by the standards of the day. The one-price policy initiated by David Lubin in 1874 was also no longer an oddity. In fact, given the expansion of retail businesses across the country, the policy was a necessity and therefore adopted widely. Initially touted, as Lubin did in early newspaper ads, as a "guarantee of justice and equity in pricing," fixed pricing became the only practical means by which a store with many employees could do business. As historian Susan Porter Benson noted, the 120 or so salespeople at Macy's in 1875 could not be trusted to negotiate prices individually on behalf of the entire store. Also, as sales volume increased, the act of negotiating each transaction would slow

Lettering on the glass display case of women's fashions says, "Weinstock-Lubin, Importers." Salesmen in the fabric department wait on women seated at the counter. Circa 1891.

the rate of sales considerably. Additionally, department stores were carrying an increasingly vast array of consumer products that had not been part of everyday life in the past but were fast becoming essential to developing and maintaining a lifestyle. The customer had to somehow be told the value of these items, and price was one way of doing that. Porcelain, crystal and clothing took on new meaning, and fashion assumed greater importance.[5]

There was also a distinct employee culture at Weinstock, Lubin. In addition to the profitsharing plans established in the late 1880s, Weinstock, Lubin & Co. instituted a number of other amenities meant to enhance the well-being of its employees—what one reporter called "David Lubin's dream of dignity for all human beings." During this era, department stores hired grade school–aged children to work as cash boys and girls, running back and forth between the selling counters and the cashier's desk with customers' payments and change. Children who worked at Weinstock, Lubin were required to spend several hours a day in the store's school, time for which they were paid. Female employees were driven home by a chaperone if no one had called for them at closing time. It was these types of policies that fostered a sense of closeness among employees and made for staff that stayed on in employ of the store for several years or many decades. Little

Employees of the Big White Store gather for a photograph. This is believed to be the store's opening day, 1891.

Pearl Labhard, who had performed daily for one week as the dancing fairy in the Big White Store's main display window in 1891, returned a few years later to work as a sales clerk in the glove department. There were also social events produced for employees, a subsidized lunchroom, a summer retreat at Ben Lomand in the Santa Cruz Mountains purchased by the company for use by the employees and public recognition for years of service rendered to Weinstock, Lubin & Co.[6]

A Broken-Hearted Man

Only two years after the opening of the Big White Store, David Lubin was less involved with the company's day-to-day management and increasingly engaged with his work in agriculture. In keeping with his personality, Lubin's fight against the tariff and for the interests of small farmers was all-consuming, and the price paid was the very public and humiliating ending of David and Louisa Lubin's marriage a few years later. David Lubin had married native Californian Louisa Lorraine Lyons in San Francisco shortly after he opened the Mechanics' Store in Sacramento. They had six children (five of whom survived), community standing and a successful business. Now, twenty years later, their marriage ended abruptly.

Details of the 1896 divorce appeared in San Francisco and Sacramento newspapers in merciless detail.

There was a tacit agreement that the papers would not publish any information about the divorce until May 11, after David Lubin had left Sacramento with his five children for an extended trip to Europe. But the *San Francisco Call* and the *San Francisco Chronicle* hit the streets the day before with screaming headlines sure to draw the public's attention:

LUBIN SEEKS A DIVORCE
Papers Filed in Which His
Wife Is Charged With
Adultery
Ex-Mayor Steinman Named as Co-respondent—The Complainant a
Well-Known Merchant

The *Call* noted that Louisa Lubin's "objectionable conduct" had been going on for three years, but it was only recently that David Lubin had acquired enough evidence, through reports from detectives following his wife, to file for divorce. Former Sacramento mayor B.U. Steinman, a longtime family acquaintance, was named in the divorce suit.[7]

Once the *Chronicle* and the *Call* published their accounts, the *Bee* followed suit with a front-page story. A reporter spoke with Lubin at his home as final preparations were made to whisk the children out of town and away from the publicity. "Mr. Lubin…seemed to be a broken-hearted man, whose soul had been entered by the iron," the reporter wrote. The *Chronicle* had given details of Louisa's wooing and downfall; the *Bee* repeated those details, noting that Sacramento's former mayor had "made the first move toward winning his friend's wife. He began by making her presents of French novels, and little by little, he added to these novels others of a lower and lower moral tone." When Steinman eventually asked Louisa to leave her husband and children and go away with him, she went to her husband and told him what had happened. Although he forgave her, the affair continued. "Gradually," the *Bee* reporter noted, "the couple became bolder and their visits to each other more frequent." One of the illicit lovers' favorite meeting places was the Grand Hotel in San Francisco, but there were other meeting places as well, including the Lubin home in Sacramento on occasions when David Lubin was out of town, the home of a friend on Eighth Street in Sacramento and a house at 1621 H Street.[8]

In an unguarded moment, Lubin explained to the *Bee* reporter how he had forgiven Louisa after her initial confession and how things had progressed from that point:

> *I discovered this woman's unfaithfulness and I condoned the offense and we went on living together. One time she came to me and she said that if I did not love her voluntarily she could not care for me. She said that she did not want to be loved from a sense of duty. I could not love her as I had, knowing what I knew, and I told her so, but still there was no rupture.*

But once the detectives presented the evidence of Louisa's continued meetings in San Francisco, and the servants in the Lubin home began to suspect what was happening and reported their suspicions to David Lubin, he confronted her with the new information.[9]

Louisa, the *Bee* reported, was "completely overwhelmed at the evidence which he had against her." She then broke down and confessed, detailing the times, places and circumstances of her assignations with Steinman. She asked for no mercy, made no objection to the divorce and would make no defense against the action. Louisa Lubin had reportedly been the recent recipient of a sizeable inheritance from her mother. In addition, the *Bee* reported that she was given $25,000 by her husband with the promise of an additional $100 per month.[10]

"Regarding the man who has brought me this great trouble I have nothing to say," Lubin stated. "Were I a younger man I would probably have done some rash act, but that period is passed and nothing should be said about this matter whatsoever." At that point in the interview, the reporter noted, Lubin left the room and joined his children, who were "playing amongst the ruins of the back parlor."[11]

Lubin never spoke publicly against his wife and asked that nothing harsh be said against her in the newspapers:

> *This woman has been my wife for twenty years. She is the mother of my children. Why should I besmirch her? Why should I give the public any information in regard to the acts of this woman? I found her out in her wrong-doing and we have agreed to part. She will go her way and I will go mine. Go: Publish that—simply that we have agreed to part, for that is all the public should know.[12]*

David Lubin took his five children and went to Europe. Little is known about Louisa after the divorce. She left Sacramento and went to her brother's home in Michigan but eventually moved to Denver, Colorado. In 1900, she was still living in Denver. The $25,000 David Lubin gave her at the time of the divorce would be worth approximately $657,000 in 2011 dollars. That coupled with whatever sum her mother left her and the $100 per month agreed upon in the settlement would have left Louisa comfortably set and able to, presumably, afford her own household. According to the 1899 Denver city directory, Louisa appeared to have been living alone.

DAVID LUBIN'S CHANGING ROLE

The unraveling of his marriage, the humiliation of the divorce and the strain of dealing with the tariff issue had left Lubin exhausted and suffering from stress. His doctor recommended that he immediately stop work, but rather than rest while in Europe, Lubin continued to broaden his crusade on behalf of small farmers. While in Budapest for the celebration of Hungary's 1,000[th] anniversary, he was invited to attend an international congress convening to discuss the causes and remedies of the decline in the world's price of farm staples. Although delegates came from many countries, the United States was not represented, and Lubin did not attend in an official capacity. Invited to attend by the Hungarian minister of agriculture, Lubin delivered what turned out to be the first outline of the future International Institute of Agriculture.[13]

Returning to the United States in December 1896, Lubin took up residence in Philadelphia. Newly elected president William McKinley had let it be known that one of the first tasks of his administration would be a revision of the tariff. As Lubin continued to fight for equal protection for both U.S. manufacturers and agricultural concerns, he became very well known in Pennsylvania, particularly among the various religious denominations that supported his message. A delegation of five clergymen delivered the Lubin proposal to President McKinley, reminding the president that he had already pledged to carefully study it. Lubin's efforts, however, went down to defeat, and the Dingley Tariff Bill passed in 1897 without the equities for which the Lubin group had hoped. Rather than represent the end of Lubin's agricultural endeavors, the education he received during the tariff fight broadened his vision. He determined to take his fight for the farmers back to the world stage. While in Philadelphia, he met and married the much younger Florence Platnauer, and by the end of 1897, the couple—along with Lubin's children from his first marriage—had returned to California and set up residence in San Francisco.[14]

With David back on the West Coast, Weinstock, Lubin & Co. began to think about further expansion. The Big White Store was doing well, and in 1898 the company opened an additional store in San Francisco at the corner of Taylor and Market Streets. A new corporation was formed for the San Francisco store. Initially managed by David Lubin, the reins of the San Francisco site were soon turned over to Edward Bonnheim, a relative who had long been a member of the Weinstock, Lubin organization. Florence, meanwhile, gave birth to daughter Dorothy, and David began work on his book, *Let There Be Light*. Published in 1900, *Let There Be Light* was Lubin's philosophical endeavor for the common man. He addressed his book not to scholars but to "thoughtful men and women of all classes," promoting the idea that there are universal laws that lead to right action.[15] Lubin's entire focus was now on his crusade to instill a new philosophy and foster reform. He would never again take a direct hand in the day-to-day operations of Weinstock, Lubin & Co.

"THE LOSS SEEMED APPALLING": DISASTER STRIKES THE BIG WHITE STORE

When the 1891 store opened, it seemed that the directors of Weinstock, Lubin & Co. had greatly overestimated the growth potential of Sacramento. A mere five years later, however, they found it necessary to build an annex at the rear of the building covering an area of 60 by 160 feet and reaching from the basement upward to all three stories. By 1900, even more space was needed; another 80 by 160 feet were added west of the annex, and an additional 60 by 160 feet were added to the eastern side. These additions matched the levels of the basement and first floor only. By 1901, the company had acquired an additional 40 feet fronting K Street, and by the close of 1901, the Big White Store covered 180 feet along K Street and 200 feet along L Street and was 320 feet deep. In all, the store measured 136,000 square feet, employed a minimum of four hundred and a maximum of seven hundred people and, by 1903, had sales amounting to $1.5 million. A minor flood (the year is not noted) created problems and

A street scene near Fourth and K Streets, circa 1900. Weinstock, Lubin & Co. is on the right. *Courtesy of the Center for Sacramento History, David Joslyn Collection.*

was responsible for some loss of merchandise; a greater disaster, however, was yet to strike.[16]

At approximately 4:00 a.m. on January 31, 1903, a fire broke out. An official Weinstock, Lubin account of the fire written one year later noted, "At the time of the fire the store was as near our ideal of what a business institution of the kind should be as we knew how to make it. When it was swept away within a few hours, the loss seemed appalling, and at first thought irretrievable."[17]

The fire started in the annex, and although the store maintained its own small fire company on the premises, the men were unable to fight the initial fire because of the "suffocating smoke." It appears that, believing they could fight the fire themselves and assuming the fire would be contained to the annex, the private fire crew did not immediately call in the alarm. The annex, connected to the main store via a bridge spanning the alley, was an elaborate structure. The bridge provided an easy access point for the fire, and it "roared furiously through the tunnel and was soon spreading along the galleries in the main building." Because the main building of the store had no interior walls, the fire took hold very quickly. A system of barred iron doors securing the building kept the city's firemen from gaining access, and the heat generated by the blaze soon became overpowering. Hundreds of

The fire that struck during the early morning hours of January 31, 1903, destroyed the Big White Store. This corner was the only recognizable section of the building left.

spectators had gathered outside but were soon driven to the opposite side of the street as the large plate glass windows cracked and shattered one by one. Fire rolled out and upward through the openings where the display windows had been. The heat from the fire scorched and blistered buildings half a block away, and spectators had to move even farther back, able to get no nearer the heat than one block. A newspaper reporter on the scene described what happened next: "With a thunderous roar the roof of the white building, 160x160 feet square, caved into the mass of flame. Then the beholders were transfixed by such a sight as comes to most men not oftener than once in a lifetime. A column of flame rose to the heavens fully 300 feet." One witness who watched from his home five miles away from the fire said the flames rose higher than the dome of the state capitol.[18]

In just three hours, the Big White Store was gone; all that remained was an archway and the bay above it at the corner of Fourth and K Streets. This was deemed so unstable that a crew was quickly put to work to pull it down. Witnesses at the scene noted that the water supply to fight the fire was woefully inadequate and that the fire hose ran mud for some time when it was turned on. Even when water did flow, it was so loaded with mud that

The fire reduced the Weinstock, Lubin & Co. store to rubble. The collapse of a wall during the blaze killed one firefighter and injured others. *Courtesy of the Center for Sacramento History, Helen Astill Collection.*

the water fell far short of where it was aimed. But when questioned about the water supply by a reporter, Harris Weinstock stated that the supply was adequate, and he had no complaint to make regarding the work of the city's firemen. "The fire was beyond control," he said. "The firemen did heroic work—reckless in the extreme, and I regret the accident that resulted." The accident to which Harris referred was the death of fireman Frank Casebolt, whose skull was crushed when one wall of the building fell.[19]

The directors of the company convened on the morning of the fire, and it was Harris who spoke for them. They would rebuild: "We propose to take off our coats and go to work with more energy than ever. Four hundred people have been thrown out of work by this catastrophe, and our purpose is to give them employment again just as soon as we can." Many Sacramento businesses, including competing merchants, stepped up with offers of space to use and any other help they could extend. The chamber of commerce and its members began collecting pledges of money earmarked to aid

Hundreds of spectators gathered to watch the fire and were driven to the opposite side of the street when the large plate glass windows of the Big White Store began to crack and shatter one by one. In the aftermath of the fire, many Sacramentans came by to view the damage.

the families of those injured or killed fighting the fire. Among the largest contributors to the fund by far were competitor Hale Bros. & Company, furniture manufacturer John Breuner Company and the National Bank of D.O. Mills.[20]

The Sacramento fire was such a huge story that the *New York Times* picked it up the following day. By full daylight on January 31, the store "was a mass of rubbish and smoking ashes." Early estimates of the loss were set at $600,000, and insurance amounted to only $400,000. The large vault housed in the store's basement and buried under the rubble of the collapsed building was dug out the following day. There was concern that perhaps the safe was not truly fireproof. But when a hole was cut in the side, the store's ledgers, cash books, minutes of the board of directors' earliest meetings and other valuable items were found intact.[21]

The store's safe was buried under the rubble of the collapsed building. Among the important ledgers and documents inside were the minutes of the board of directors' earliest meetings. These meeting minutes, intact with the exception of their burnt edges, are preserved as part of the Weinstock-Lubin Collection. *Courtesy of the Center for Sacramento History, Helen Astill Collection.*

Thanks to the availability of temporary quarters at the Old Pavilion on the corner of Sixth and M Streets, the department store did not miss a beat. Makeshift shelves and counters were put in place, and merchandise arriving at the freight station was rerouted to the new location. Buyers dispatched to San Francisco intercepted incoming goods, unpacked them and rapidly got them to a state of readiness for the store. On the morning of February 9, "when the ruins of the fire were still smoking," the temporary site of Weinstock, Lubin & Co. opened for business. In a show of support, Sacramentans came to the temporary store and purchased $1,800 worth of goods on the first day. For almost four months, business was conducted in the awkward facility. Departments such as furniture and carpeting had to be left out of the building entirely. Still, sales were equal to 80 percent of the corresponding months for the previous year. By June 1, 1903, an annex at Fourth and K Streets had been completed. The makeshift operation closed at the temporary location on Friday evening, May 29; on Monday morning, June 1, less than five months after the fire, the company "threw open the doors

For approximately five months following the fire, Weinstock, Lubin & Co. operated out of temporary headquarters at the corner of Sixth and M Streets.

of the new annex ready for business." Weinstock, Lubin & Co. continued to work out of the annex, operating without show windows and requiring patrons to approach the K Street entrance over a "long, wooden, unsightly canvass covered bridge 180 feet long." Counters were made of unpainted pine, and the surroundings were quite rough; still, the store succeeded in continuing to hold sales at 80 percent of the previous year's business.[22]

Although the loss of the Big White Store was devastating, a department store fire in this era was not unusual. Historian Jan Whitaker notes that from the 1890s until World War I, stores burned regularly, some under somewhat suspicious circumstances. Most stores that burned, Whitaker states, "came back bigger and better after they received their insurance settlements." The Weinstock, Lubin fire does not appear to have been a case of insurance fraud, and the cause was theorized to be the spontaneous combustion of oily rags thrown carelessly by some furniture packers into a large amount of packing material in the basement of the annex. It was noted in the *Bee*, however, that agents of several of the insurance companies that covered the store had long considered the Weinstock, Lubin property to be a dangerous risk. With each annex and extension to the building, the rate for coverage had been raised.[23]

On June 11, 1903—fewer than five months after the fire—contracts were let for the rebuilding of the main store. The plan for the new Weinstock, Lubin & Co. building, including the annex, totaled 178,000 square feet.[24]

THE BIG WHITE STORE RISES AGAIN

Thirteen months after the fire, the new Weinstock, Lubin & Co. opened its doors on the same spot at Fourth and K Streets. The new Big White Store was fully one-third larger than the store that burned. Opening its doors on February 29, 1904, the company touted the new building's "perfect system of heating and forced ventilation" for shopping comfort in both cold and warm weather, a wider assortment of merchandise, an increased buying force in New York and shipments of goods from Europe. For the employees, there were clean, light-filled rooms designated for lunch, reading and school and a new kitchen to serve the staff.[25]

When the cornerstone of the new store was laid, a five-page letter by Harris Weinstock was placed inside it. In addition to describing the fire, recovery and rebuilding, Weinstock also speculated on the progress that would be made before the letter ever again saw the light of day. In contrast

A new and larger Big White Store opened its doors at Fourth and K Streets on February 29, 1904. Circa 1915.

to the more lyrical musings of employee Alice Haley, who wrote an essay that was placed into the cornerstone of the 1891 building, Weinstock's letter placed in the 1904 cornerstone was more grounded in its tone and practical in its musings. Perhaps the events of the previous year had given the Colonel, at least temporarily, a more subdued manner.[26]

III

A New Generation and a
World at War,
1904-1919

*If ever the history of this great revolution in human affairs that may now
be in progress should come to be written, there must be at least a vignette of
the prophetic American Jew, David Lubin.*
—*H.G. Wells,* The World of William Clissold

Eight months after the new store opened, David Lubin returned to Europe. By 1904, his ideas on a more scientific system of distribution for the world's agricultural products had crystallized into a plan, and he lost no time in putting all his resources into achieving a hearing of his ideas. Some doubtless considered Lubin to be quite mad; others regarded him as something of an annoyance at the least and a political problem at the worst. If change were going to occur, he reasoned, it must come from the top. He put himself in front of as many heads of state as he could. Kings, presidents, emperors—David Lubin had no problem approaching people in positions of power. His ideas about agriculture had been met with hostility in Washington, and his position on the tariff received considerable attention and drew the ire of his own political party. As a Republican, Lubin believed in a protectionist position as a way of aiding American industries, but he could not reconcile that position with the plight it caused the farmers. By the time of his divorce from Louisa in the spring of 1896, both political parties were preparing for the upcoming presidential election, and what had come to be called "Lubinism" was now a recognized issue. Lubin's failed efforts at influencing President McKinley following that election made him determined to seek a hearing on the world stage.[1]

Lubin was absolutely convinced that all he had to do was state his ideas clearly to the right people—those who possessed a vision to match his own and the power and resources to make that vision a reality. He failed to make any headway in Washington, London or Paris. In 1905, he made his way to Rome. Although he was unable to speak a word of Italian, Lubin succeeded in securing an audience with Italy's king, Victor Emmanuel III. Lubin's idea, developed with the help of his son Simon, was for a sort of international chamber of commerce that could give farmers the kind of international market information and technical assistance that could only be provided with the cooperation of governments. Of course, Lubin did not simply ask for and receive an audience with the king. Using an interpreter—Olivia Agresti, who became his friend, co-worker and biographer—Lubin approached a series of Italian officials. While the minister of agriculture quickly dismissed Lubin's ideas as too American, the young head of the Labor Bureau of the Ministry of Agriculture, Industry and Commerce, Giovanni Montemartini, saw otherwise. Believing that what Lubin had to say was significant, Montemartini enlisted the support of veteran statesman and minister of the treasury Luigi Luzzatti. Sufficiently impressed with Lubin's proposal, Luzzatti gave Lubin a letter of introduction so that he might request an audience with the king. There were a few miscues along the way, but eventually David Lubin, the one-time proprietor of a ten- by twelve-foot one-price dry goods store in Sacramento, had secured an audience with King Victor Emmanuel III.[2]

The result was a May 1905 world conference held in Rome and attended by high-ranking emissaries from forty-one countries. Its singular goal was to hammer out plans for a global organization that would collect, study and publish information on farming. In order to bolster attendance at the conference, Lubin traveled throughout Europe, encouraging heads of state to participate in the conference, both as a courtesy to the Italian king and as a vehicle for advancing their own causes. One of Lubin's goals was to take control of agricultural production and prices away from international speculators, and appealing to governments to become directly involved was one way of doing this. The largely self-educated Lubin succeeded in convincing the international congress of his plan. As Harris Weinstock wrote some years later, Lubin "found himself faced with some of the keenest living intellects—faced by men, many of them who had enjoyed the world's biggest and best educational advantages. Few men's minds and few men's ideas ever were subjected to a test so keen." The end result was the inauguration of the International Institute of Agriculture (IIA), headquartered in Rome and housed in a beautiful palace built with the private funds of King Victor Emmanuel. Reportedly, U.S. secretary of agriculture James Wilson was incensed that this outsider had stepped into his world and usurped his role. Secretary Wilson so despised Lubin that Washington would have refused the invitation to attend the international conference had the issue not been taken up by Secretary of State John Hay and President Theodore Roosevelt, both of whom viewed the issue as a diplomatic, not an agricultural, one.[3]

Lubin's lack of diplomacy and what appeared to be his disinterest in both protocol and outright politeness made him seem arrogant to some and admirable to others. Lacking patience with those who did not immediately share his vision, David Lubin put his mission ahead of everything else. It is no wonder he has been described in near-biblical terms. Writer H.G. Wells, who met Lubin in 1916 and maintained their friendship via correspondence until Lubin's death, described the visionary as having "the burning eye and the gestures and intonations of a major prophet...This crazy-mannered, posturing, one-price merchant had a real Mission, and was doing a work of the utmost significance."[4]

Lubin had spent a considerable amount of his personal fortune to see the institute come to fruition, but he was certainly not a pauper. Weinstock, Lubin & Co. continued to function well without him, so his finances were secure.

While Lubin devoted all his energies to the work of the IIA and his appointment as America's permanent delegate to the institute, Weinstock divided his time between managing the store and engaging in his own civic duties. In 1908, Harris Weinstock was appointed state labor commissioner, and the position afforded him the opportunity to travel extensively throughout Europe, Russia, Japan, China, Korea and India studying labor conditions. An author like his half brother, Weinstock published two books during this period: *Jesus the Jew* and *Strikes and Lockouts*. Weinstock's experience with agriculture on the state level led to his appointment in 1915 as the state market commissioner, an office that later became the California Department of Food and Agriculture.[5]

Weinstock, Lubin & Co. had become firmly established as an enterprise that reflected the progressive ideas of its founders, and those ideas gained traction outside the business as well. Now a new generation prepared to step into the family business.

Family Expectations

David Lubin and Harris Weinstock expected much of their children. David and Louisa Lubin had six children, three boys and three girls. While daughters Ruth, Laura and Eva did not enter the family business, they were expected to become well educated and take on social responsibilities. Opportunities abounded for the Lubin and Weinstock children. While accompanying her father through Europe, Laura Lubin worked as a *New York Times* correspondent; Eva Lubin, the youngest of David and Louisa's children, married Italian Count Silenzie and remained in Europe. Because son Albert died at the age of six, expectations of entering the family business—regardless of other interests—fell to oldest son, Simon, and his brother, Jesse. Weinstock's sons Walter and Robert each launched careers as top managers, even though neither one of them wanted to be in the family business. Robert never considered himself to be a businessman, and Walter wanted to be a writer.

David Lubin held his children from his marriage to Florence Platnauer to the same rigid expectations regarding their educations, yet their career paths did not take them through the Sacramento department store. Daughters Dorothy Lubin Heller and Grace Lubin Finesinger both attended Bryn Mawr College in Philadelphia, Pennsylvania; Dorothy went on to earn her medical degree from Johns Hopkins University Medical School while Grace earned her PhD in chemistry and physics at Johns Hopkins. Dr. Heller practiced medicine at clinics in New Jersey, and Dr. Finesinger became well known for her research contributions to understanding syphilis and

David Lubin's three youngest children (left to right): Grace, Teddy and Dorothy, circa 1908. After his divorce from Louisa Lyons Lubin, David Lubin met and married Florence Platnauer.

pneumonia and for her development of mental health centers. Theodore (Teddy) Lubin, the youngest of David Lubin's children, became a stockbroker in England.[6] Thus, of the eight surviving Lubin children, the weight of maintaining and building the family business interests fell largely to Simon and Jesse Lubin.

More than any of the other Lubin children, Simon had thoroughly grasped his father's agricultural mission. Simon was more comfortable with that aspect of his father's work than with the department store and real estate enterprises. Rather than study business management, Simon had studied economics and philosophy and graduated summa cum laude from Harvard. In the few years following graduation, Simon made four trips to Europe to study problems of race, nationality, international migrations, agricultural marketing and people's daily lives. His work proved extremely useful to his father, and David Lubin used much of Simon's research in constructing his plans for the IIA. Once the institute was established, Simon helped his father prepare various projects considered by the IIA.[7] In 1906, Simon returned to Sacramento and began to work at Weinstock, Lubin & Co., which was still being run by Harris Weinstock. By the time Simon Lubin entered the family business, the Big White Store had unquestionably become the center for fashion in Sacramento.

THE FASHION CENTER OF SACRAMENTO

The new Big White Store at Fourth and K Streets had become *the* style setter for Sacramento. Where the 1881–82 Weinstock, Lubin mail-order catalogue described skirts simply as one of three styles—walking, demi-train or full train—clothing was now understood more in terms of fashion, and middle-class women looked to department stores and magazines to educate them as to what was fashionable and how to wear it.

A February 1911 newspaper ad for Weinstock, Lubin featured gorgeous illustrations of fashionable hats from Paris. The "Millinery Exposition for Spring" boasted French creations from several designers, all named in the ad with the intent of either informing the fashionable where works of known designers could be found or educating a willing audience of fashion neophytes that the designers were names to know and their creations were prizes to be sought. The ad also referred to hats from "leading American designers" but did not single out those designers by name. The store promised that "newness, unequalled interest, and Foreign ideas will be the all-prevailing

The Weinstock, Lubin & Co. store at Fourth and K Streets decorated with lights for the 1905 Street Fair. *Courtesy of the Center for Sacramento History, Eugene Hepting Collection.*

Interior of the Fourth and K Street store, circa 1915.

features of this remarkable *Exposition des Modeles, Saison D'Été*, 1911" and used a new slogan in the ad: "The Fashion Center of Sacramento." A follow-up ad produced to look like a newspaper article and appearing the day after the event said the exposition surpassed visitor expectations. "Throngs" came to see "exclusive ideas," and overheard amidst the conversation was the comment, "Weinstock, Lubin & Co. does things just like a New York store." The new spring styles were housed in the store's French Room, and women were encouraged to stop by and look, even if they did not intend to buy. "The chief value of this opening," the ad copy read, "is in the style knowledge you gain."[8] Weinstock, Lubin & Co. strove to be the center of Sacramento's fashion universe.

Service at the department store was an individualized experience with one-on-one attention the norm. Nowhere was this more evident than in the time-consuming, intricate process of fitting a customer for a pair of very fashionable French kid gloves. The customer sat on a revolving stool at the glove counter, her elbow propped on a velvet cushion. First, the glove was measured around the clenched fist. Then, each finger of the glove was measured against the customer's fingers. Talcum powder was blown into the glove and rubbed on the customer's hand. The customer's elbow was bent at an angle to provide leverage for the slow pressure that eased the glove along the fingers and onto the entire hand, then the glove was snapped or buttoned at the wrist with the aid of a small button hook. The final step in the process was to admire the end result.[9] Sacramento's women had—quite literally—all they could desire in fashion right at their gloved fingertips.

CHANGES IN LEADERSHIP AND STORE POLICY

In 1911, the board of directors voted Harry Thorp president of the company. Thorp had begun his association with Weinstock, Lubin & Co. years before as a clerk in the store. His hard work and developing expertise led to his rapid advancement in the company. As president, however, he faced challenges for which he was not fully equipped.

In his February 1912 report to the stockholders of Weinstock, Lubin & Co., Thorp referred to difficulties of the preceding year in general terms as he noted, "Throughout the past year a national unrest existed all over the United States bordering so closely on a depression that trade was hampered, and more or less pessimism was in the atmosphere." Labor unrest, immigration and Americanization concerns and economic issues had all taken their toll; nationwide, there was a concerted attempt by business to control a labor force estimated to be as much as 60 percent immigrant, strikes in the decade of 1910 were at record levels and the 1911 Triangle Shirtwaist Factory fire in New York that killed 146 people drew greater public attention to the conditions of workers and the message of trade unions. Thorp noted that in Sacramento there had been "strikes and rumors of strikes which kept our own people in constant fear, and restrained their buying tendencies."[10]

To the public, however, Thorp distributed a much more reassuring message. Following a March 1912 trip back east, he told the press only positive things, like about his meeting with inventor Thomas Edison, and he provided reporters with a somewhat rosier economic outlook. "Trade conditions in New York are good," he told a reporter. "There is no evidence of a depression and no prospect of a boom, so I look upon this as a normal condition which in my judgment forecasts a healthy general business for 1912." Much closer to home, the greatest concern for the firm was the trend toward businesses in Sacramento moving "up-town"—eastward away from the river and toward the capital. Buildings erected near Eighth Street such as the Peoples Bank and direct competitor Hale Bros. department store, in addition to the location of the terminal for two important electric trolley lines, all served to steer business away from Fourth and K Streets, rendering the up-town location Sacramento's new "shopping center." The trend eastward was one that the board of directors had clearly missed. "Looking backwards," Thorp reported,

> we seem to have completely overlooked this up-town development, otherwise an effort would have been made to counteract this move by some outward signs of life [by improving] our K Street property, or equipping [our store] with conspicuous electric advertising signs...We must do something additional to keep this end of town attractive and interesting.[11]

Concern about the changing retail landscape in Sacramento drove many of the company's business decisions for the next several years.

A WORLD AT WAR

In 1914, when war broke out in Europe, David Lubin was in Washington, D.C. Lubin and his daughter Dorothy left Rome for Washington just prior to the assassination of the Austro-Hungarian Empire's Archduke Franz Ferdinand and his wife in Sarajevo. Lubin had come to Washington to promote his idea for an International Commerce Commission for the regulation and control of ocean freight rates and to meet with the Senate Banking and Currency Committee about a rural credits bill that was being drafted. But as war intervened, Lubin realized those issues would be largely pushed aside by Washington. He was determined to continue the work of the International Institute of Agriculture (IIA); however, as the war escalated, food issues grew worse.[12]

Returning to Rome in December 1914, Lubin actively participated in the work of the IIA's permanent committee. The committee met regularly, with delegates from Germany, Austria, Hungary and Turkey still functioning as active members. Committee members may have been able to continue to function together despite their countries being at war or allied with other committee members' countries, but the IIA was still hit hard by the hostilities. The international staff had been depleted by war mobilization in their own countries.[13]

A display at the main entrance of the Big White Store, part of Weinstock-Lubin's World War I war effort, encouraged Sacramentans to save food. Circa 1917.

With the sinking of the *Lusitania* in May 1915, Lubin's focus shifted. He had no doubt that the outrage felt by the people of the United States over the deaths of 128 Americans—citizens of an officially neutral country—would result in United States entry into the conflict. It did not happen. While Lubin continued to maintain an officially neutral organization in the IIA, he realized the significance of the war and the importance of the struggle. On his next trip to the United States, Lubin did not talk about international freight or rural credits; he spoke instead on national defense and the need for military and economic preparedness.[14]

In 1916, President Woodrow Wilson won reelection using the campaign slogan, "He kept us out of the war"; yet in April 1917, America entered the conflict.

WEINSTOCK, LUBIN AND THE WAR EFFORT

For the Weinstock, Lubin & Co. employees and management who remained on the job during the war, there was still much to be done. The department store gave a $3,034 check to the American Red Cross in 1917, a sum large enough to warrant the front page in a local newspaper. This money, it was noted in the article, was separate from any money employees of the store donated or raised on their own. The local chapter of the American Red Cross had set a fundraising goal of $75,000 to $80,000, and it used the Weinstock, Lubin donation as a springboard for publicly announcing hopes that every merchant in Sacramento would contribute. In addition to donating funds for the cause, the store used its display windows to support the war effort and promote patriotism on the homefront. And in response to an announcement that the lack of available ships meant all packages to soldiers in the American Expeditionary Forces in Europe would be refused unless they were sent upon a request countersigned by a company commander, Weinstock, Lubin put together a system that allowed packages from families to get to soldiers at the front. The department store took orders for gifts and then sent those orders to Paris, where the goods could be purchased and sent to the front without the need for transatlantic shipping. No profit was made on the transaction; the customer was charged the Paris price for the goods plus the express service from Paris to the front. The store also assigned one employee—Miss Mott—to coordinate the service. Mott provided lists of items soldiers wanted along with the current Paris price list, and she noted that "one may send everything from handkerchiefs,

This "Crush the Kaiser" World War I display window encouraged Weinstock, Lubin customers to buy war savings stamps to help Uncle Sam and "our boys." Circa 1917.

A potato-cooking demonstration held in the store was part of an effort to encourage Sacramentans to eat the surplus crop of potatoes and to conserve other agricultural products like beef and wheat. Circa 1917.

trench lamps, sleeping bags, sweaters and socks, to glace fruits, candies, cakes, roast chickens, meat and soup."[15]

But the company was also looking toward the future, and the future was not in the neighborhood of Fourth and K Streets. Sacramento's business district had been moving steadily eastward, away from the riverfront and toward the capitol. Other retailers had already established a foothold in the area and had cost Weinstock, Lubin customers. Hale Brothers built its store at Ninth and K Streets well before the war, and its marketing efforts had steadily drawn business toward the location, eventually shifting the entire central business district.[16]

Plans for a new Weinstock, Lubin store splashed across the front page of the *Sacramento Bee* in November 1917. The new store would require a $1,000,000 investment and was planned for the corner of Ninth and L Streets. The initial design called for a ten-story department store with a frontage of 210 feet on L Street and 100 feet on Ninth, giving a ground area of 33,000 square feet. The estimated gross square footage of the building was 336,000 square feet—158,000 square feet larger than the current Big White Store. Display windows would line two sides of the building, and Weinstock, Lubin president S.W. McKim announced his intent to make it one of the most attractive department stores in America. McKim had traveled to all the large American cities to gather ideas and had worked with several of what he considered to be the best architects in the country to come up with the design. "The store," the article read, "is to be a monument to business integrity and a beacon by which to steer trade in Sacramento from the entire Sacramento and San Joaquin Valleys." It was also the first of the company's planned expansions to consider the existence of the automobile, although at the time it did not consider that automobile ownership would grow to large numbers.[17]

The Ninth and L Street location was selected, apparently, because it was *not* on the streetcar line but near to it. Citing that one family in every three owned an automobile, the company determined that shoppers would prefer to drive to the store on a street unhampered by streetcars. Ideas such as this played out in major shopping districts across the country. In the early days of automobile ownership, department stores determined that the well-to-do would shop more often in department stores because they could travel to the store's doorstep in their own automobiles. Setting aside large areas for parking did not enter into any design plans, as it was assumed automobile ownership would not mushroom beyond its present state. But by the early 1920s, merchants saw the increase in automobiles as something of a curse as the flood of automobile traffic in downtowns across the country pointed out the lack of curbside parking and precipitated unpopular parking restrictions.[18] Over the next two years, plans for the new store changed.

By 1919, the site for the "Million-Dollar Store" had been moved to Eleventh and J Streets. This would take the store even farther eastward into new retail territory. Transportation again figured into the shift. Stating that the J Street site had the advantage of streetcar connections with all districts and would be within a short distance of the interurban transportation lines, newly elected chairman of the board Simon J. Lubin stated that this district would be the center of Sacramento's retail zone. The future of the property at Ninth and L Streets acquired under the leadership of S.W. McKim was still undecided, but McKim's future was not. In a massive reorganization of the business just two months prior to the announcement of the new site, McKim retired, and a new management structure was put in place. A ten-member board of managers, composed entirely of store employees, was now part of the store's decision-making process.[19] With Simon as chairman of the board, a Lubin was once again at the helm of the business ship; his brother, Jesse Lubin, was now mail-order manager.

The announcement of the building site change sent ripples through the local real estate market, and this new purchase of half a block by the local retailer had come as a complete surprise. In addition to the J Street property, Weinstock, Lubin bought additional property on I Street. In response, several real estate companies took options on property in the vicinity of the announced building sites, believing that other big structures would be planned for that district within a short time. Other businesses also leapt at the opportunity to establish a foothold in what looked to be the new central business district of a growing Sacramento. Don Lee, a Bay Area automobile dealer who would later establish one of the earliest regional broadcast radio networks in the United States, announced his intention to build a $200,000 garage and automobile sales room at Twelfth and H Streets.[20]

On New Year's Eve 1919, the *Sacramento Bee* announced that plans for the big department store were completed and construction would begin in early February 1920. Now scaled back to eight stories instead of the original ten-story concept, the new store would feature two public entrances (one on J Street and the other on Eleventh Street), several high-speed traction elevators, spacious public tearooms and a grill, a cafeteria for employees where food would be served to them at cost, a large employee club room and employee exercise facilities on the roof.[21] This turned out to be another store design the public would never see come to fruition.

"THIS WAS AS DAVID LUBIN WOULD HAVE WISHED IT"

On November 25, 1918, David Lubin drew up a resolution that was unanimously adopted by the IIA's Permanent Committee. Calling attention to the IIA's ability to assist with the development of the League of Nations, the resolution called on the adhering governments to bring this information to the attention of the Versailles conference to settle the war. Versailles was also where President Wilson hoped to establish the league.[22]

It was the last Permanent Committee meeting Lubin attended. He died in Rome on January 1, 1919, another of the numerous victims of the influenza epidemic that ravaged country after country. His daughter Dorothy remembered, "I was told by Mother that Father was scheduled to accompany President Wilson on his ride through Rome, January 1, 1919. He had been looking forward to this honor with great pleasure, because he greatly respected Wilson. Father's death that same day deprived him of this honor." When David Lubin's will was filed for probate in New York two months later, it was reported that he had left the bulk of his $600,000 estate to his widow and children. Additional bequests included $1,000 to start a fund for a national academy of music for African Americans and $1,000 to the Hebrew Union College of Cincinnati. The national academy of music was a concept he had first put forth in his book *Let There Be Light*, calling it "a practical beginning in the domain of highest achievement."[23] Lubin had always held both music and learning in the highest regard.

Simon Lubin attended his father's funeral in Rome. In addition to the dignitaries present were a representative of the king of Italy and the mayor of Rome. Simon had requested that the flags of both the United States and Italy drape his father's coffin, and on the procession to the Jewish Cemetery "every passerby paid his respects by raising his hat. The women made the sign of the cross and the soldiers stood at attention." Affixed to the back of the hearse, a large floral arrangement from the king bore the royal blue ribbon reading, "Vittorio Emmanuele." As his friend and biographer Olivia Agresti noted, in the excitement of President Wilson's arrival in Rome, the United States Embassy forgot to send a representative to the funeral, and the floral tribute from the king of Italy was the only official recognition of David Lubin's long life of service. "With the same simplicity with which he had lived, this pioneer of organized international life went to his well-earned rest. And this was as David Lubin would have wished it."[24]

A RETURN TO NORMALCY

During his 1919 campaign, Republican presidential candidate Warren G. Harding promised the nation "a return to normalcy." For department stores like Weinstock, Lubin, "normalcy" meant adjusting how they did business. Prices rose during the war and its immediate aftermath as soldiers returned home and demand increased for still-scarce goods. Nationally, the cost of living more than doubled between 1914 and 1919, hitting its peak in the immediate postwar period. As the economic situation stabilized, people began to indulge in a desire for "happy, feel-good merchandise." American toymakers in particular benefitted in the war's aftermath. When the war in Europe began in 1914, about half the toys sold in the United States were manufactured in Germany. A number of Americans boycotted German imports, and when the United States entered the war, importation of German goods stopped altogether. American toy makers moved toward year-round production by the end of the war, and their products now included dollhouses,

Santa's arrival was the start of the Christmas season at Weinstock, Lubin, and Santa arrived at the store in different ways. In 1918, he arrived in Sacramento by submarine.

pedal cars, electric trains, stuffed animals, kites and more. Department stores like New York's Lord & Taylor made the unprecedented move to year-round toy departments in 1919 and 1920.[25]

The emphasis on happiness, normalcy and a chance to feel good in the wake of the Great War was especially evident in Weinstock, Lubin's advertising campaign for Christmas 1919. Incorporating an enthusiasm for airplanes that grew out of the war, along with the childhood excitement of Santa's annual visit, the store ran a series of delightful newspaper ads tracking the progress of Santa Claus on his way to Sacramento for the big Santa parade and Santa's reception at the store. Each day, a new "aerogram" from Santa to "Messrs. Weinstock, Lubin & Co." was made public in the newspaper so that eager children could track Santa's progress. In the first communication, Santa noted that as he was getting ready to leave for Sacramento, his "reindeers took sick," so he had to build "an aeroplane to carry me away from the land of the frozen North." He said that Weinstock, Lubin has his advance shipment of toys, which should last until his arrival. The next day's message found Santa with a loaded plane and on his way at last. "If I do not have an accident I shall be with you by Saturday." Santa's next message was sent from Seattle, Washington. "Stopped at Seattle just long enough to take on more gas. Had an exciting race with a wild seagull today." The children of Seattle wanted him to stop, of course, but he told them he had promised to come straight to Sacramento. On Friday, November 14, the headline over Santa's message read: "Santa Claus will arrive by aeroplane to-morrow about 10 a.m." Santa's final aerogram was sent from Mt. Shasta, California:

> *TELL CHILDREN I AM ON VERY LAST LAP OF MY LONG, COLD RIDE FROM LAND OF THE FROZEN NORTH. EXPECT TO REACH SACRAMENTO ABOUT 10 A.M. SATURDAY MORNING. SHALL FLY OVER CITY AND INSPECT CONDITION OF ALL CHIMNEYS IN SACRAMENTO. WILL THEN PARADE UP J STREET AND DOWN K STREET TO STORE WHERE I SHALL HOLD RECEPTION. TELL CHILDREN I EXPECT THEM TO BE DOWN AT SOUTHERN PACIFIC BRIDGE AT 10:30 TO SEE ME COME IN.*
> *S. CLAUS*[26]

The war was over, there was a promise of prosperity and Santa Claus was coming to town—a return to normalcy, indeed.

IV
"PARIS" COMES TO SACRAMENTO,
1920-1945

We can say in all modesty that ours is not just an ordinary store building.
To the contrary it is perhaps without exception at this moment the most
modern department store structure in America.
—Weinstock, Lubin & Co.

With the war over and the public's desire to buy unleashed, Sacramentans began to hear more rumors of a new and bigger store to replace the longtime fixture of Weinstock, Lubin & Co. at Fourth and K Streets.

While that site had held the large department store from its 1874 beginnings as a small dry goods establishment through the first Big White Store, the ruinous fire and the second, even larger Big White Store, it had become obvious to the board of directors that any further expansion would necessitate a departure from its historic location. In April 1920, the company sold off two pieces of K Street property between Fourth and Fifth Streets. Later that month, the wrecking ball was set to work on the recently vacated buildings at J Street between Eleventh and Twelfth Streets, site of the "new $1,000,000 department store."[1]

By May 1920, Weinstock, Lubin & Co. was ready to begin excavation of the site for its new store. The site at Eleventh and J Streets had been cleared; the only thing holding up the excavation work was the building permit still to be issued by city building inspector Ben Covell. Covell and the Weinstock, Lubin engineers had held several conferences, and according to a May 22 published report in the *Sacramento Bee* attributed to Simon J. Lubin, president of the company, "good progress was being made and the architects and engineers now are waiting for the permit to proceed with the construction work." Other newspapers reported that ground had already been broken on the new project.[2] Two days later, the entire enterprise ground to a halt.

The new building project had been postponed indefinitely, and it appeared that stories of the groundbreaking were unauthorized. The reason cited by Weinstock, Lubin for the postponement was "the present economic and unsettled conditions affecting both the financial and mercantile world." The company's engineers had indeed been in talks with city building inspector Bill Covell about securing the building permits, but the decision to halt the project was reached suddenly. With Simon Lubin out of town for a month, research manager C.W. Bryant served as spokesman for the department store. He was quick to point out that the decision had nothing to do with the financial condition of the department store itself—Weinstock, Lubin & Co., he noted, was today "stronger financially than when the plans first were laid for the new store." At issue, he noted, was "the action of the banks in pulling down the highly inflated credits…and the nation-wide movement to reduce prices in retail lines while the wholesale and jobbing houses are holding fast." The new consumer goods industries of the early twentieth century had allowed Americans to enjoy the highest standard of living of any country, but a brief postwar depression created a financial environment that led to scenarios such as this—indefinite postponement of business expansion. Weinstock, Lubin & Co. was confident the situation was only temporary. "It may be a week, a month, or more," Bryant noted. "Just as soon as conditions become more settled something definite as to when work will start can be expected."[3]

Speculation continued to swirl about the new store for the next two years. Rumors of an alliance with the California State Life Insurance Company for joint occupation of a five-story building at Ninth and L Streets and reports that a San Francisco real estate investment company had purchased the Fourth and K Street building that was still home to the department store kept the buying public and Weinstock, Lubin's competitors guessing as to where the Sacramento retail giant would finally land.[4]

Decisions made by the department store carried a great amount of weight with a great many people, from real estate companies looking at a store move as an indicator of retail land values wherever Weinstock, Lubin decided to move to consumers looking to the store for advice in matters of taste and fashion.

Weinstock, Lubin & Co. may have been just a local department store, but its founders and the new generation of Lubins and Weinstocks had been long used to wielding considerable influence within the community and in local government as state commission appointees. Their actions and opinions carried some weight in many quarters but not, it seems, in the editorial offices of the *Sacramento Bee*.

"ONE OF THE MOST HORRIBLE PICTURES WE HAVE EVER SEEN IN ANY NEWSPAPER"

In the summer of 1920, at the age of twenty-nine, Carlos McClatchy, son of *Sacramento Bee* editor C.K. McClatchy and a respected journalist in his own right, ran the editorial side of the *Bee* while his parents and sister Eleanor were on a twenty-two-month trip through Africa, the Mediterranean and Western Europe. On the front page of the December 10 edition of the newspaper, Carlos published a graphic image showing the lynching of three "gangsters" who had been jailed for killing three police officers. Acquiring the photo in time for publication was a technical feat in itself, for the lynching had occurred in Santa Rosa in the early morning hours of December 10. The photo that Carlos ran in the *Bee* had to be taken by flashlight and sent by airplane to Sacramento's Mather Field so that the *Bee* would be able to run it on the front page of that evening's edition.[5]

As it happened, the Friday, December 10 edition of the *Sacramento Bee* also included a Weinstock, Lubin & Co. Christmas advertisement aimed at children—an invitation to a doll reception hosted by Santa Claus and Goldilocks. The department store board, led by Simon Lubin, was furious at the gruesome photo on the newspaper's front page. In protest, Weinstock, Lubin ran an apology ad in the December 13 editions of the *Sacramento Bee* and the *Sacramento Star*, as well as in the December 12 edition of the *Sacramento Union*, that said, in part:

> *In our desire to reach the public, we strive to have our advertisements enter the homes of the city. Realizing that we cannot be successful in achieving this if the media we use are unclean or unwholesome, we have, from time to time, protested to the papers if they placed undesirable matter in the same issue in which our advertisements appeared...Our advertisement in the* Evening Bee *of last Friday was a special appeal*

to children. On the front page of the same issue there was published a photograph of a lynching—one of the most horrible pictures we have ever seen in any newspaper. We feel that no child should have seen that picture, and we regret that in appealing to the children of the city we were probably instrumental in increasing the number of those who were subjected to such a gross indignity.[6]

Carlos McClatchy accepted the Weinstock, Lubin ad in the *Bee*, allowing the open criticism, but also ran an editorial that left no doubt in readers' minds that advertisers do not control the content of the *Bee* and that even the largest advertisers in the newspaper did not determine the news. McClatchy also noted that "pictures of far more ghastly subjects were published during the war" and that other newspapers critical of the lynching photo "ran in all its gory details the picture of the bomb outrage on Wall Street [referring to the September 16, 1920 bombing that killed thirty-eight and injured more than one hundred others], the scene of thirty bodies mangled and spattered on the surrounding walls":

This department store, which has departments ranging from millinery to pins, through departments of How to Run A City, What's Wrong With Sacramento, and the Do As I Say department, seems now to have added another on Newspaper Censorship. Weinstock-Lubin as a commercial store is an efficient institution. Sacramento, however, has declined with thanks the invitation for her affairs to be run by that store and evaded with difficulty the attempts to do so.[7]

Not to be outdone, the department store replied in the December 14 editions of all three newspapers:

We welcome the opportunity the Bee*'s editorial gives to reiterate the opinion we expressed in the above Apology; and we are perfectly willing to leave it to the public of Sacramento to decide which of the two attitudes supports decency.*[8]

After both sides made their points, the dust settled, but not before the *Sacramento Union* weighed in with a small article that appears to have been the last word in this particular battle. In reporting that a man who claimed to be representing the *San Francisco Call* newspaper was arrested for selling picture postcards of the Santa Rosa lynching on the street outside the

Federal Building, the *Union* closed the article by stating, "One of the leading physicians of Sacramento yesterday said that as a result of being confronted with the gruesome picture, several women were under his care."[9] One imagines the ladies under the doctor's care following shocking exposure to the lynching photo postcard to be middle class and middle-aged. The emerging "new woman" now being constructed in motion pictures and showing up on college campuses would likely not have succumbed to any sort of nervous collapse over the postcard. She had a different sensibility, and department stores—among others—needed to pay attention.

THE YOUTH MARKET AND DEPARTMENT STORES

Department stores had come to view themselves as a primary source for fashion information; customers relied on department stores like Weinstock, Lubin to keep them current. Most of the store's regular customers likely had not traveled far afield in their lives. Weinstock, Lubin executives and buyers made trips not only to the major retail centers of the Midwest and East Coast but to Europe as well. Until this time, "style" unquestioningly came from Paris and filtered down to the masses through the wealthy elite. But after World War I, more independent ideas about style and fashion were filtering through the culture, especially among the young. The trend had already begun in the early twentieth century, as young women used what was available to them to create new looks. This might include starching their collars to extremely high points, wearing considerably more jewelry than was considered tasteful by social matrons, pushing up their sleeves or simply using color in ways not previously seen in fashion. Department stores, of course, did not consider these "looks" to be fashion's leading edge and so did not take advantage of changes in fashion the young women who worked in the stores were creating or the changes in social attitudes they were mirroring.[10]

That idea was changing rapidly as the young—a market that had been largely ignored—began to demand more attention. Weinstock, Lubin, just like other department stores and established institutions across the country, was faced with a cultural shift as the nation's youth—particularly young women—changed, and genteel sensibilities as to what appeared in the newspapers or what constituted appropriate fashions were questioned. Department stores had to acknowledge this new cultural sensibility or risk losing this emerging youth market.

Recognizing that Sacramento's business district had shifted, Bishop Patrick Keane of the Diocese of Sacramento sold the Christian Brothers School at Twelfth and K Streets, shown here, to Weinstock, Lubin. Circa 1923.

A LITTLE BIT OF PARIS ON K STREET

After years of speculation and rumored property deals, a move for Weinstock, Lubin & Co. became official in 1923. The Fourth and K Street property, sold two years prior to prepare for the move and leased back by the department store since that time, had been deemed "undesirable for a large retail establishment" owing to its proximity to what had now become Sacramento's wholesale district. The retail center of Sacramento had been gradually shifting eastward. Now, Weinstock, Lubin was about to shift with it.[11]

Plans for the new store included a full basement and three floors above ground, with the option to add two more stories at a later date. Construction costs were estimated at $850,000; the total investment including land and the building was expected to reach $1,250,000. The store would occupy the southwest corner of Twelfth and K Streets, with 240 feet along K Street and 160 feet along Twelfth Street. This

Construction on the Twelfth and K Street store began in early June 1923. The diocese agreed to end the school term on June 1 rather than June 23 so that demolition could begin as soon as possible. Excavation of the new department store's basement began shortly thereafter. Circa 1923.

announcement followed closely on the news that a new ten-story, "Class A" hotel—the Hotel Senator—would be built at a cost of $1,500,000 at Twelfth and L Streets, just behind the new Weinstock, Lubin store and one block away from the grounds of the state capitol. The property for the department store, situated kitty-corner from the Cathedral of the Blessed Sacrament, was the current site of Christian Brothers School. Bishop Patrick Keane, appointed to bishop just one year before, offered the aging Christian Brothers School building and land for sale in recognition of the shift in Sacramento's business development. For Keane, the real estate transaction meant the opportunity not only to facilitate Sacramento's urban growth but also to improve Catholic education with a new location for an improved school. As part of the deal with Weinstock, Lubin, Keane agreed to cut the spring 1923 term short from June 23 to June 1 in order to give immediate possession of the property to the new owner so that demolition could begin.[12]

Financing for the construction followed a modern trend. During the early 1920s, many department store companies issued mortgage bonds as a means of generating funds needed for construction. Through these means, stores could grow based on business projections rather than on actual sales. Simon Lubin approached the San Francisco bond house of Branford Kimball & Co. A June 28, 1923 telegram from Branford Kimball to Simon Lubin noted the wide interest shown in the bond offering: "The confidence shown in this issue by security buyers we consider the highest testimony of the esteem in which Weinstock Lubin and Co. are held by the public at large."[13]

The design for the new store was also very much part of a national trend in department store modernization. In the 1920s, department store exteriors exhibited a French-inspired modernism, emphasizing long banks of display windows and centrally placed entrances. The Weinstock, Lubin design was based on the Parisian department store Le Printemps and featured a terra cotta and marble finish on the structure's exterior and a grand, centrally placed entrance facing K Street. The building was designed so that windows could be placed at "every available point, assuring plenty of light and air." Show windows, of course, figured prominently in the design. By October 1923, the public and store employees had begun to get a taste of what was to come via regular reports of construction progress. Passersby who came to see the huge construction project read updates on a "News Bulletin" board attached to the construction fencing surrounding the structure. Information regarding the new home of the Christian Brothers School was also posted. Updates under the heading "New Building News" appeared in the store's newsletter and in advertising. Sacramentans kept informed about the site's excavation and the reinforced concrete used, the modernity of the ventilation system being installed, modern methods to cool the building, a sprinkler system and methods of lighting. Employees were given special construction updates that included information regarding the new "airy, well-ventilated locker rooms, clinic with nurse's quarters, a silence room where women may rest, [and] a reading room and a smoking room for men where cards, checkers or reading may be used to enliven the lunch hour period." Plans called for four large elevators—three for the public and one for freight—operated with machinery in the roof's penthouse rather than by noisy equipment in the basement; drinking fountains, men's and women's restrooms, a barbershop, a children's playroom, a

This page: As the construction of the new store progressed, Sacramentans could read the project updates on a "News Bulletin" board posted on the construction fence. Circa 1924.

hair salon and a beauty shop were also among the features of the new department store. As construction proceeded, Simon Lubin set Monday, June 2, 1924, for the store's opening.[14]

All merchandise at the Fourth and K Street location had to be moved across town to the new site. The move was set up like a military operation. Because of the magnitude of the job, no one company was used for the project. The work was distributed among a number of moving companies based on the type of equipment they had and the capacity of their trucks. C.H. Hailes, store superintendent, and H.S. Bailey, director of moving, coordinated the operation. Divisions were created consisting of various departments; under these were smaller units. Each unit had a forwarding agent at the old store to check out the goods and a receiving agent at the new store to check in the goods. The Sacramento Police Department and special detectives provided security to guard against theft and interference of bystanders. In an effort to reduce the amount of stock that had to be moved, the store held a "Removal Sale" beginning on Monday, May 9, at 9:00 a.m. Billed as "A Good Buy Sale at Fourth

On opening day, June 2, 1924, crowds of people stood in line, hoping to be among the first to see the new store. The day had been set aside as an informal public reception. All departments were open for inspection, but no merchandise was sold on that day.

The first visitors in line press against the main doors as Simon J. Lubin, the son of David Lubin, and a woman presumed to be Barbara Weinstock, the widow of Harris Weinstock, unlock the doors for the grand opening.

and K," the public were encouraged to take advantage of management's desire to "start the new store new."[15]

On Thursday, May 29, former U.S. representative Grove L. Johnson—father of former governor and U.S. senator Hiram Johnson and a longtime friend of founders David Lubin and Harris Weinstock—ceremoniously locked the doors of the store at Fourth and K Streets for the last time. The doors to the new store at Twelfth and K Streets were thrown open by Simon J. Lubin at 3:00 p.m. on Monday, June 2. As the doors were opened, the show windows on both K and Twelfth Streets were unveiled. The crowds of men and women who had been lined up for hours streamed in. The day was set aside as an informal public reception. All parts of the store were open for inspection, with members of the staff on hand to greet the public and help familiarize them with the store, but absolutely no merchandise was sold on opening day. Numerous floral arrangements arrived at the store from other department stores, manufacturers and retail merchants in Los Angeles, San Francisco, Oakland, Portland, Chicago,

New York, Boston and other cities. Large crowds attended the reception, which continued until 10:00 p.m. that evening.[16]

A new era in retailing had begun in Sacramento.

The Most Modern Department Store Structure in America

Opening just four months before Weinstock, Lubin & Co.'s fiftieth anniversary, the store at Twelfth and K Streets was considered a marvel. At the time, the location was referred to by management as "the place where the busiest street in Sacramento meets the Lincoln Highway"; to others, it was "practically out in the country." Most agreed, however, that it was a beautiful and amazing structure. The exterior had columns and facings of cream-colored terra cotta tile, and an enormous,

Large floral arrangements and best wishes for the opening arrived at Weinstock, Lubin from department stores, manufacturers and retail merchants throughout the country.

custom-made terra cotta medallion by pioneering ceramics company Gladding-McBean of Lincoln, California, provided a grand touch to the main entrance. Upon entering the main archway, one walked across a black-and-white-trimmed gray terrazzo floor. The mezzanine, which ran completely around the main floor, was considered an impressive architectural innovation for its time and created a "feeling of openness and spaciousness no matter at what point on the main floor or mezzanine one may happen to be." The top floor of the building was known as the "Fashion Floor." Covered from end to end in one great, dark blue rug, the top floor offered a luxurious setting for the display of women's coats, suits and millinery. "We can say in all modesty that ours is not just an ordinary store building," store management noted in a souvenir fiftieth-anniversary booklet. "To the contrary it is perhaps without exception at this moment the most modern department store structure in America."[17]

The new store was designed to be highly functional, as well as stunningly beautiful. Almost all the store fixtures were new and had been

The light, open interior was just one aspect of the modernity of the new Weinstock, Lubin department store.

designed specifically for the Twelfth and K store. The fixture system was built to be movable and interchangeable, and specialty displays were designed based on research and experimentation undertaken in other department stores across the country. Artificial lighting supplemented the natural light that flooded the building during the daylight hours rather than substitute for it. The modern ventilation system drew 100,000 cubic feet of air into the ventilating shaft every minute, an amount deemed sufficient to change the air completely in the entire building four times an hour. The ventilation system "washed" the air by drawing it through jets of water, then humidity was corrected and the air was circulated into the store either in its cooled state or heated. Air of different temperatures could be delivered to different floors at the same time. In addition to the technical marvels of the new department store, some of the offerings inside were modern, as well. An American Express Travel Bureau on the mezzanine level could take care of customers' travel needs from general information to securing theater tickets. Other new departments making

One of the most popular features of the Twelfth and K Street store was the lunch counter. Patrons waiting to dine would "stake out" a spot behind someone already seated at the counter in hopes of being the next diner to occupy the seat. Circa 1940.

their appearance in 1924 included crockery and glassware, a circulating library, a golf shop, a soda fountain and lunch counter and a special department for men's work clothing.[18]

When Christmas came to the Twelfth and K Street store, it was indeed spectacular. Employee Ethel Geiss remembers, "We were taught when the doors to the store opened, it was the same as opening the doors of our home." The customer was a guest and was treated accordingly. Employees who had worked at Fourth and K were amazed at the new store and for decades after remembered how Santa Claus filled the alcove above the main door on K Street. The display windows were filled with animated dolls, electric trains, beautifully dressed mannequins and gorgeous decorations.[19]

By 1926, plans for more intensive merchandising led Simon Lubin to seek additional capital; at the same time, Weinstock, Lubin & Co. filed new articles of incorporation for the purpose of changing the company name by adding "Inc." Along with the capitalization, Lubin made an announcement through the press that the only change occurring was the addition of "incorporated" to the name of the company. There would be no changes in personnel, management or policy.[20]

The new store at Twelfth and K Streets featured an electric sign. Circa 1925.

Sacramento's Finest Department Store

By the mid-1920s, Sacramento's department stores were credited with making Sacramento a retail shopping hub. In addition to the new Weinstock, Lubin Twelfth and K store, the relocated central business district included major competitor Hale Brothers, just up the street at Ninth and K. The San Jose–based Hale Brothers opened its first Sacramento store in 1880—a mere six years after David Lubin first hung out his One Price sign—and had been direct competition ever since. Hale's expansion to half a block of Eighth and Ninth Streets along K occurred one year before the big Weinstock, Lubin opening. Also located in the region were the Charles P. Nathan Co. and women's specialty store the Nonpareil. There were national chain stores, as well, including Montgomery Ward & Co. and Sears, Roebuck & Co. According to 1927 chamber of commerce statistics, Sacramento retail businesses had an annual retail payroll of $7,584,000 and employed 5,120 people.[21]

This page and next: Paramount Pictures actress Edna Kirby lived for one week in her "Glass House, Apartment Unique" in the Weinstock, Lubin display windows. She performed this publicity stunt at other department stores as well. Here she is seen dining, sleeping and playing the piano in front of curious passersby. She appeared in the window each day from 10:00 a.m. to 9:00 p.m. Circa 1925.

A headline in the October 12, 1929 *Sacramento Bee* declared, "DEPARTMENT STORES BOOM CITY AS RETAIL SHOPPING CENTER." Twelve days later, share prices on the New York Stock Exchange fell abruptly on "Black Thursday," and the country began to head into an economic downturn.

DOWNTURN, CHANGES AND RECOVERY

The Depression was not a deathblow for department stores, and in reality, no major department stores closed during the 1930s. By 1936, most were able to return to the sales volumes they had generated before the stock market crash. But the industry itself—and the role of department stores—changed. Historian Jan Whitaker theorized that the department store as an institution might have been very different had it not been for the Depression. She notes that in the 1920s, the stores were headed in the direction of "sophisticated European-style worldliness." The opulence and attention to detail in Weinstock, Lubin's Twelfth and K Street location bears this out. Even the building was intentionally modeled after a famous Parisian department store. But, as Whitaker notes, everything changed, and although department stores survived the Depression better than small shops, adjustments had to be made. Instead of linking themselves so closely with European style, department stores across the country moved to be more in tune with mainstream American culture. They promoted American products, included more brand names in their stores and even sought promotional ties with Hollywood.[22]

For Weinstock, Lubin, the 1930s were marked by legal as well as economic issues, significant management changes and loss of the final ties to the store's founders.

By 1932, Simon Lubin had left his position as president of Weinstock, Lubin. As director of the California Department of Commerce—a position to which he was appointed by Governor James Rolph—he moved his offices and his home to San Francisco. New Weinstock, Lubin president Lawrence Ellis began his tenure at the top by attempting to instill confidence in Sacramento's buying public. In February of that year, Ellis made a spring buying trip back east. Upon his return, he told reporters that "a little more optimism is manifest among businessmen on the Atlantic seaboard."[23]

In spite of the Depression and the change in leadership, Weinstock, Lubin continued to hold huge parties for employees in honor of the store's birthday.

Crowds gather for a back-to-school promotion, circa 1931.

Employees who worked fifteen or more years were always honored at these events, and both management and employees had significant involvement in each year's program. In 1933, at the fifty-ninth birthday celebration of the store, the 350 employees in attendance at the annual banquet surprised Ellis with a large floral NRA (National Recovery Administration) emblem, signifying the addition of sixty-five employees to the company's roster since the NRA's Blue Eagle banner appeared at Weinstock, Lubin. Under the NRA plan, all companies complying by rehiring workers at minimum wages could place a Blue Eagle on their products and businesses. This was a way for the public to support those business concerns working to create employment and purchasing power in the United States. Carrying the motto "We Do Our Part," the NRA Blue Eagle flew early at Weinstock, Lubin.[24]

A new challenge arose as one of California's oldest department stores prepared to celebrate its sixtieth anniversary in 1934. Rival Hale Brothers bought two promissory notes of the Weinstock, Lubin Company held by the now closed California National Bank. The two notes totaled $123,000, but Hale Brothers bought them for $60,000. An attorney for Hale Brothers had presented an offer to the bank's receiver to purchase the notes. The petition by Hale explained that an examination of the condition of Weinstock, Lubin on September 30, 1933, showed assets of $637,235.50, but it was estimated that not more than 50 percent of those assets could be realized on a quick liquidation.[25] The old competitor now held a chunk of its rival's assets.

Perhaps one of the most poignant losses for the city of Sacramento during the Great Depression was the disappearance of the Big White Store. Shortly after Weinstock, Lubin's sixtieth anniversary celebration, the bank that owned the iconic structure at Fourth and K Streets announced that the building was to be razed so the lot on which it sat could be sold. Citing the "inability to obtain a sufficient number of profitable leases on the building," tenants were given notice to vacate, and the demolition began shortly thereafter. Several months later, a copper box laid in the cornerstone of the building in 1903—the same copper box that had been placed in the cornerstone of the 1891 building that had burned at that spot—was unearthed. Inside were a 1903 letter from Harris Weinstock written for the new cornerstone, the documents that had been placed inside the box for the 1891 ceremony and a selection of newspapers from 1891 and 1903. The five-page letter signed by Harris Weinstock recounted a brief history of the business but went into detail about the 1903 fire. Weinstock took great pains to acknowledge those in the community who came to their aid both during the fire and in its aftermath as the business was trying to rebuild. He reserved the final paragraphs of his letter for some prophetic statements about the future growth of California and the life to be enjoyed by its populace. His one miscalculation: "Neither the writer, nor any of those now living who are connected with the business, expect ever again to see this document after it is once deposited in the box to be placed in the corner stone." Charles E. Phipps, who at one time had been vice-president of the company, was the only executive of the original store still living. He had participated in the laying of both the 1891 and 1903 cornerstones and was present with company president Lawrence Ellis as the box was opened in 1935.[26]

It does not appear that Simon Lubin made the trip from San Francisco to be present for the opening of the cornerstone box, a circumstance that seems to confirm he was completely removed from the business that his father, David Lubin, established in 1874. Although he had resigned his post as chief of the state's bureau of commerce amid talk of an ouster, in 1936 he became associated with the California State Relief Administration as a consultant. Ill health forced him to retire from active business quite suddenly that same year, and in March he died at the age of fifty-nine of what was listed simply as a "chronic ailment." His younger brother, Jesse, always much more in the background, remained with Weinstock, Lubin only four more years, until his retirement. In 1957, Jesse Lubin committed suicide at the age of seventy-two because of poor health.[27]

Both the Weinstock, Lubin and Hale Brothers department stores began rebounding and in 1936 made front-page news when they announced that employees of both stores would receive cash bonuses amounting to 5 percent of their total wages for that year. Bonuses were scheduled to be paid to regular employees on December 18. Executives for both stores noted that the bonuses were intended to show appreciation for "the loyalty and efficient and faithful services of the employees." The bonuses were not given to company executives or to those working on a commission basis. George Conover, manager of Hale's, and Lawrence Ellis, now being listed as manager of Weinstock's, notified employees of each company in separate meetings but presented the same message: their hope that conditions would justify making the practice an annual one.[28]

Even in the department store's earliest days under David Lubin's active participation, Weinstock, Lubin never shied away from consistent,

The Weinstock, Lubin store was a prominent fixture on K Street. Circa 1936.

aggressive—even innovative—advertising and store promotions. In the late 1930s, the department store began its own radio show on McClatchy-owned radio station KFBK. Called *Woman's Reporter of the Air*, the program aired Saturdays at 9:15 a.m., immediately after the morning news broadcast. The radio show was promoted in the store's newspaper ads, reminding newspaper readers to tune in to the broadcast. Another promotional draw that attracted shoppers in the late 1930s were the "Miracle Windows" at the Twelfth and K store. Operating on a technology called "Teletouch" developed by Leon Theremin, inventor of one of the first electronic musical instruments—the theremin—the windows used a beam of light extending across part of the sidewalk. When a pedestrian crossed the beam, the display windows would illuminate for thirty seconds. The store's newspaper ad promoted the windows as an entertainment: "Now they're ON, now they're OFF…more fun and mystery and modern achievement! As you approach, the windows [three of them] are dark, while one lone eerie light beam flows across the sidewalk. You pass the beam…ON go the radiant white lights for 30 seconds…and OFF again till another passerby!" The Miracle Windows operated from 7:30 to 11:00 p.m. nightly on the K Street side of the store. The windows attracted enough attention that an article appeared in the newspaper about them, explaining Theremin's invention in some detail.[29] Other advances and store improvements were in the planning stages, but with the United States' entry into World War II, further changes to the store at Twelfth and K were shelved indefinitely.

WEINSTOCK'S AND THE WAR

As was the case during World War I, Weinstock, Lubin management and employees participated fully in community efforts during World War II. With many of the store's personnel in the armed forces and the curtailed production of civilian commodities, rationing, scarcity and transportation problems were part of daily life, and it was difficult to continue to supply the people of Sacramento with even basic items. According to the department store's postwar 1949 seventy-fifth-anniversary souvenir booklet, the company proudly noted that throughout the war it adhered "strictly to the government's price control and economic policy" and "contributed in every way possible to maintenance of home front morale by supporting every phase of the War Loan Drives, by educating

Weinstock, Lubin & Co. and its employees led many efforts on the homefront during World War II. Here, students from the Marshall School knit blankets and other articles for the war effort. The knitting instructor, Agnes Kreisel, was employed by Weinstock, Lubin. Circa 1942.

consumers in the care and use of substitute materials and by supporting all community and national welfare drives such as Community Chest, Red Cross, U.S.O. and March of Dimes." The United States Treasury and the army and navy also cited the department store on numerous occasions for its advertisements and window and interior displays that promoted those community drives.[30]

Not all wartime activities could be touted so loudly. Following America's entry into the war after the December 7, 1941 attack by Japanese forces on the American Pacific fleet at Pearl Harbor, the management of Weinstock, Lubin issued a statement to its employees regarding Japanese Americans. The December 10, 1941 memo advised that, in order to use a check, Japanese customers had to present both birth certificates showing they were U.S. citizens and official documents from their banks stating that banking officials confirmed their accounts were for personal use only. A follow-up memo on December 19 clarified new Treasury Department regulations concerning wages and living expenses for Japanese nationals. A check for

Display windows frequently featured campaigns encouraging the purchase of war bonds. In this display, the public is reminded that even America could lose a war. Circa 1943.

payment had to be accompanied by a "certificate or some document" showing that the customer was either a U.S. citizen or had resided within the United States since June 17, 1940. Checks could not be drawn on Japanese banks; only checks from United States banks would be accepted. At this time, almost five thousand Japanese Americans lived in the region, and the actions of Weinstock, Lubin were in keeping with California policy. Within three months of President Roosevelt's signature on Executive Order 9066, Sacramento's Japanese American population was evacuated to internment camps for the duration of the war.[31]

Although David Lubin, the department store's founder, had died at the end of the last world war, his contributions on the world stage had

In the days following the June 6, 1944 D-Day invasion of Normandy, France, Weinstock, Lubin and Sacramento radio station **KFBK** broadcast military bands from the store's main corner display window. The music was part of an effort to sell Bonds of the Invasion.

not been forgotten. In 1944, a Liberty ship bearing his name—the SS *David Lubin*—was launched from the Richmond Shipyard in California. As a gift to the captain and crew of the ship, the Lubin family provided a portrait of David Lubin to be installed on the ship, a combination radio and record player, a record cabinet and one hundred records for the enjoyment of all onboard. Also in 1944, Californians received word via newspaper reports that the International Institute of Agriculture (IIA) had been left untouched by Fascist and Nazi authorities during the occupation of Rome. All property, including the archives of the institute, was safe; the diplomatic immunity of the IIA had not been withdrawn, and the IIA's research was allowed to continue.[32]

During the war, a *Sacramento Bee* photographer captured the stunning image of an enormous American flag unfurled over the main entrance of Weinstock, Lubin & Co. The store's participation in bond drives and newspaper ads

During World War II, Weinstock, Lubin flew the American flag prominently over the main entrance. The department store's newspaper ad on Flag Day in 1944 reminded Sacramentans not to take their flag for granted: "Fly your colors this Flag Day—and every day till Victory. Buy Bonds to Speed that Victory."

encouraging Sacramentans to fly the flag took the place of much of the advertising focused on merchandise. As World War II drew to a close and American servicemen returned home, there was a strong, understandable desire to return to normal. But the postwar period would bring significant changes of its own, to both Weinstock, Lubin and Sacramento.

V

SUBURBIA, SPRAWL AND A WOMAN AT THE HELM, 1946-1973

The store's responsibility does not end with the sale of merchandise, but should also be directed to the general welfare of the community of which it is a part.
—*Marion Armstrong, President, Weinstock, Lubin*

The end of the war brought new expansion for the Sacramento area. People who had come west for defense-related employment chose, in many cases, to make California their permanent home. In 1940, Sacramento County had a population of 170,333; by 1950, that figure had jumped to 277,140, an almost 63 percent increase and the largest increase in the county over a ten-year period since the gold rush era. Key industries in the region included three military installations: the Sacramento Signal Depot, which functioned as a large army supply and repair center for military communications equipment; McClellan Air Force Base, one of the largest air force supply and maintenance bases in the United States; and Mather Air Force Base, which served as an important training site. Local, state and federal government, as well as manufacturing, provided much of the employment opportunities for Sacramentans.[1]

The end of the war saw not only a shift in population distribution but also the release of a pent-up consumer demand. Housing issues were a primary feature of postwar America, but most developers, at least initially, were not much concerned with where the residents of their newly built suburban homes would work and shop. By contrast, Sacramento-area home builder Jere Strizek paid attention to this issue early on. He opened Town & Country Village at the corner of Fulton and Marconi Avenues in 1946. One of the first major shopping centers in Sacramento County, Town & Country Village was positioned to take advantage of the new residential growth in the region.[2] In the next few years, this suburban lifestyle, of which the automobile was a key component, would have a tremendous impact on the decisions made by Sacramento's retail businesses.

In spite of changes in the residential landscape and the early development of new consumer options, department stores still held sway in the public mind as arbiters of style and taste. In the postwar period, consumers became increasingly more brand conscious, and a "power shift" occurred between manufacturers and department stores. The quantity of brand-name merchandise in department stores grew as manufacturers' advertising created a demand for their brands. By 1950, department stores as a rule reflected broad middle-class tastes and mainstream American consumption and then positioned themselves as style authorities, current with the latest fashion trends in both clothing and home furnishings. Young postwar families just starting out in the new residential suburbs came to rely on the

Weinstock, Lubin decked out for Christmas with a large ribbon around the building's entire façade. The tag reads, "The store with the Christmas spirit." Circa 1948.

style information they received through department store brands, window displays and fashion shows.[3]

Almost as soon as the war ended, Weinstock, Lubin announced plans for expansion in early September 1945. Company president Lawrence Ellis released his ideas for postwar expansion to the press. The department store had just signed a twenty-five-year lease on the property at 1111 Eleventh Street, the building that housed the Elite Garage and the Mel-O-Dee Club cocktail lounge. The expansion, expected to add twenty-four thousand square feet of space to the store and ease space constraints in already-crowded departments, also facilitated expansion geared to serving a new postwar audience. One of the major additions was the Weinstock, Lubin & Company Youth Center. Opened in October 1946, the Youth Center cost $200,000 to build and formed the main feature in a two-year program of expansion and modernization that included the installation of escalators in the store at Twelfth and K Streets.[4]

For many, the Youth Center was a beloved feature in the store. Fixtures and furniture built in Weinstock's own carpentry and cabinet shops were scaled to size for the department store's younger customers. Department

store executives from other cities who visited the Youth Center at its informal open house claimed that it was the only department of its type in the United States. At the very least, one store executive from Los Angeles proclaimed that there was nothing else like it on the Pacific Coast. The Youth Center featured what looked like peppermint stick pillars of mosaic tiles at the Eleventh Street entrance and a milk bar scaled to size to serve small children. Sacramento native Nancy Phillips

Right and opposite page: The 1946 opening of Weinstock, Lubin's Youth Center was all about the children. Here, a young boy is interviewed and then cuts the ribbon with the help of company president Lawrence Ellis.

Below: Crowds gathered for the opening of the Youth Center. Notice the pillars that look like peppermint sticks.

ELSIE

Left: The milk bar was one of the unique features of the Youth Center. Circa 1949.

Opposite top: Escalators were an important addition to the department store as they moved far more customers from floor to floor than elevators. Circa 1947.

Opposite bottom: Although Weinstock, Lubin merged with Hales, the stores continued to operate under their own names. At this Weinstock, Lubin seventy-fifth-anniversary celebration shortly after the merger in 1949, Weinstock's employees express their sentiments in the matter.

recalled that the milk bar was "our world. It was scaled to us," she remembered, "and you did not have to have mom and dad there paying for you." It was like being a "little adult." The milk bar featured a crescent-shaped counter and little seats with everything sized for children. A store employee working behind the counter offered children their choice of white or chocolate milk.[5]

Weinstock, Lubin installed its first escalator, another key feature of the postwar expansion, in the summer of 1947. At that time, only the main floor and the basement were connected by escalator. Escalators from the main floor to the second floor and from the second floor to the third floor became operational that September. The "electric stairways," as they were called, were constructed at a cost of $275,000. Escalators were critical for moving greater numbers of people from one floor to another. Department stores had long struggled with issues of moving customers from floor to floor; customers who went to floors other than the one containing the item

for which they had come to the store would be more likely to make an impulse purchase in another department—a department they might not have visited otherwise. Escalators, depending on their size, took up one-fourth less space than elevators and carried on average twenty to twenty-five times more people.[6]

As the iconic Sacramento department store neared its seventy-fifth anniversary in 1949, a new business structure was put in place. At the August 9, 1949 meeting, the board of directors agreed to merge with Hale Brothers Stores. Weinstock, Lubin had been a partially owned subsidiary of Hale Brothers since 1930; the new transaction would merge the two corporations into one. Management assured employees that the merger was a financial transaction only and would not impact personnel, policies or procedures. Business would continue as usual with both stores operating under their own names. A memo to employees of Weinstock, Lubin noted, "We continue to do business as usual, under our own name, in the same way as always—as Sacramento's finest department store."[7]

MARION ARMSTRONG TAKES THE REINS

Remodeling of the Twelfth and K store, which began with the Eleventh Street expansion, Youth Center and the installation of escalators, continued into 1950 with the expansion of the mezzanine floor. The plans called for adding four thousand square feet by extending the balcony twenty feet out from the east and west sides over the ground-floor men's department.[8] But the biggest change came in the front office.

When Lawrence Ellis retired as president of Weinstock, Lubin, Marion Armstrong was named president of the company. Ellis, who had been head of the store for twenty-five years, retained his position as chairman of the board. Armstrong, a native of Sacramento who began her career with Weinstock's twenty-seven years before, had worked as an advertising copywriter, advertising manager and director of promotions. She had also served as executive vice-president and general merchandise manager and on the board with Ellis for several years. It was rare to find women in executive positions in department stores, and women would occupy few executive offices in American department stores before the 1960s or 1970s. Only two women became store presidents in the World War II/postwar era. Dorothy Shaver at Lord & Taylor in New York was the first woman to become president of a department store, and Marion Armstrong

This page: The arrival of Santa continued to be a grand tradition for Weinstock-Lubin. Here, crowds on K Street await Santa's arrival by helicopter. Circa 1945.

A 1955 Weinstock, Lubin Auto Show was one of many events the department store hosted as a way of attracting customers. *Courtesy of the Center for Sacramento History, Ernest Myers Collection.*

Association with celebrities, movies and television shows was another way of marketing the store and its products. These three display windows in the Youth Center offer the *I Love Lucy* infant wardrobe. The display invites parents to, "Dress your small fry like Ricky, Jr.!" Circa 1953.

at Weinstock, Lubin in Sacramento was the second.[9] As head of a store that was now part of the Broadway-Hale chain, Armstrong presided over a flurry of expansion and change as Weinstock, Lubin and Hale Brothers responded to suburban growth.

Parking was one of the first issues Armstrong tackled. Downtown business districts across the country were taken by surprise with the rapid postwar population shift from the city to the suburbs. Many department store customers lived farther away from the stores, and these customers expected to use their cars when they went shopping. According to a 1952 newspaper ad, a purchase of one dollar or more at Weinstock's got customers two hours of free parking at one of three nearby garages. But this was a short-term solution to a problem that was not going to resolve itself. In 1953, Weinstock, Lubin announced the construction of its own parking lot. Large enough to accommodate several hundred cars, the lot was located at Thirteenth and L Streets. Two buildings in the 1200 block of L Street were razed for the

As president, Marion Armstrong presided over the beginning of Weinstock, Lubin's expansion. Here, store executives including Armstrong pose on construction equipment. Circa 1957.

44,800-square-foot lot, and Weinstock, Lubin took long-term leases on the property. Only one year later, Armstrong expanded off-street parking yet again, this time by adding the southwest corner of Thirteenth and K Streets, the area formerly occupied by the used car branch of Capitol Chevrolet. The addition of the new parking area raised the total capacity of Weinstock's parking to four hundred cars. "There is heavy use of the lots," Armstrong told a meeting of the Retail Merchants Association. "The parking space not only helps our business but, we believe, the whole downtown area. We haven't restricted use of the lot to our customers and we believe all the merchants are benefitting."[10]

Although it was now part of Broadway-Hale, Weinstock, Lubin maintained a completely separate identity and its own image in the community. Sacramentans who shopped at both Weinstock's and Hale's remember each one distinctly and not as stores belonging to the same company. Weinstock's continued to set itself apart, winning national awards for window displays and newspaper advertisements and for continuing to bring a unique feature to Sacramentans: baseball. For postwar Sacramento Solons fans, baseball season meant Tony Koester, and Tony Koester meant KFBK radio and Weinstock, Lubin.

The Pacific Coast League Sacramento Solons baseball team enjoyed a broad following in Sacramento. Sportscaster Tony Koester broadcast the games over McClatchy-owned radio station KFBK. But when the team was on the road, the broadcast moved to the big display window of Weinstock, Lubin. Reading the action of the game off a ticker tape and adding his own sound effects to create the aura of a live ballgame, Koester drew large crowds to the storefront as he re-created the game for local fans. Sacramentan Gloria Glyer, herself a Weinstock, Lubin employee during the period, noted just how much fun everyone thought that was. Tony Koester sat in the window and broadcast the games, she remembered, and he did all the sound effects like the bat hitting the ball. Koester had crowd noises for background, and he would use things like two pieces of wood for the crack of the bat or slapping his leg for a pitch. It was fun, interesting and exciting, she recalled, watching Koester re-create those games right there in front of people on the street.[11]

This page: Crowds gather at the store's corner window to watch broadcaster Tony Koester re-create Sacramento Solons "away" games. Koester made his own sound effects as he broadcast the games. Circa 1950.

Urban Redevelopment and Suburban Expansion

By the mid-1950s, commercial developers across the country were building regional shopping centers with an eye toward meeting the consumer needs of suburbanites. Sacramento's suburban shopping center development began in 1946 with Town & Country Village, but as regional shopping development continued into the 1950s, a move was also afoot to revitalize downtown Sacramento and enhance the central business district. A redevelopment survey begun here in 1948 resulted in a plan that targeted areas considered blighted, in particular the blocks from the capitol westward toward the Sacramento River. The Sacramento City Council had voted to widen the boulevard between the capitol and the Tower Bridge as a way of creating a more fitting image for the thoroughfare leading to the state capitol. By 1954, fifteen square blocks had been slated to be cleared and redeveloped. San Francisco developer Ben Swig made a proposal to construct a "modern retail shopping center" in six square blocks on K Street between Second and Fifth Streets. Swig also proposed extending this shopping area seven blocks eastward, encompassing the blocks that included both Hale's and Weinstock, Lubin.[12]

Swig's plan received a mixed reception. While the city council had a generally positive response, the chamber of commerce was negative and asserted that such a plan could be implemented by local businessmen. In addition, opponents were concerned that the plan did not address issues of relocation and public housing. Two notable businesses had indicated their interest in the Swig plan. F.W. Woolworth announced that it was on board, and Sears, Roebuck, which had planned to build more on the leading edge of the urban space, indicated it would consider an alternate plan if the redevelopment proceeded. The foundering of Swig's plan—along with difficulty putting other plans together and proceeding with redevelopment—proved a boon for developers eyeing those areas outside the downtown core and catering to those Sacramentans who were primed to leave the "town center for the shopping center."[13]

As the Swig plan fell apart, Fuzz Bullock, manager of the Sacramento Sears store, began to take alternative steps for Sears's Twelfth and K Street location. Bullock invited Frank Kassis, one of the Sacramento Kassis brothers whose enterprises included the Stop-N-Shop chain of grocery stores and the Kassis Building Company, to accompany him on a ride to the north area of Sacramento's periphery. They ended up at the vacant site of Arden Way, the North Sacramento Freeway (now Highway 160) and the proposed new freeway (now I-80), and Bullock let Kassis in on some confidential information: Sears had made an overall survey of the Sacramento Metropolitan region and concluded that the cloverleaf at Arden and the freeway would be the prime focal point for establishing a new store. In short order, the Kassis brothers were invited by property owners Phillip Heraty and William Gannon to develop what would become Arden Fair shopping center. The Kassises had been asked to participate because of their retail experience. "At this time," Frank Kassis noted, "no one had been successful in selling a major department store on [the idea of] a metropolitan shopping center site." The key to the development would be the buy-in of a department store.[14]

Frank Kassis's years of service with the Community Chest meant he had made a number of contacts within the business community and was in an ideal position to approach department stores for the new venture. He met with Marion Armstrong of Weinstock, Lubin and Bill Ahern of Hale's. According to Kassis, Armstrong was cool toward the idea of expansion while Ahern was ready to move ahead, and he blamed this disagreement

The 1961 ribbon-cutting at Country Club Plaza marked the first branch location for Weinstock, Lubin. Pictured from left to right are James H. Brewer, vice-president; Prentis Hale, board member; Marion Armstrong, president; Les Wood; and Bill Ellis, store manager.

for slow progress on Arden Fair. Yet ultimately, both Armstrong and Ahern would preside over suburban expansion in near simultaneity. At a Los Angeles meeting with the Arden Fair principals and Broadway-Hale president Edward Carter, the decision was made that Hale's would go in at Arden Fair and Weinstock, Lubin would go into the new James J. Cordano development, Country Club Plaza shopping center at Watt and El Camino Avenues, a site that also included a Stop-N-Shop grocery store. Country Club Plaza was directly across Watt Avenue from another Cordano retail development, Country Club Centre. At this time, it was not uncommon for shopping centers to include a grocery store, as well as retail space. Arden Fair would proceed with Sears and Hale's as anchors and a Stop-N-Shop grocery store, too. Arden Fair would also include another Kassis creation, the Food Circus, a precursor to today's mall food courts. According to Kassis, Edward Carter had initially considered putting both Hale's *and* Weinstock's at the Arden Fair site, but Armstrong was opposed to this idea, opting instead to separate the two stores by putting Weinstock's at Country Club Plaza. The two stores opened within about five months of each other. Weinstock, Lubin opened at Country Club Plaza in March 1961, and Hale's opened its Arden Fair store—the largest in Northern California at 197,000 square feet of floor space—in August of that year.[15]

The Country Club Plaza store opened in March 1961, shortly before the opening of Hale's at Arden Fair. Circa 1967.

The opening of the Country Club Plaza Weinstock, Lubin store was also a fundraising event. The night before the March 4 opening, the Camellia Festival Association sponsored a two-hour champagne open house preview benefitting the Sutter Hospitals Auxiliary and the Mercy Children's Hospital Guild. The 1961 Camellia Queen and her princesses received the guests, corporate executives and local dignitaries. The ticketed event with about four thousand people attending raised approximately $2,000 each for the auxiliary and the guild.[16]

During this period of nationwide retail expansion—roughly 1958 through 1963—the trend showed an overwhelming decline in retail sales in central business districts across the country, while overall metropolitan sales grew 10 to 20 percent. Shoppers were very upfront about their preference for the new shopping centers over the downtown stores. Among the comments of regular shoppers were that the shopping centers were more convenient, driving and parking were easy, most of the shopping center stores had longer evening hours and the store layouts were better.[17]

THE WEST'S BIGGEST CHAIN

Sacramento was not the only expansion site for Broadway-Hale. Among the properties that the chain added in California, Broadway-Hale expanded south into the Stockton, California market. A 1962 announcement of a Weinstock, Lubin to be built at Stockton's new Weberstown development was followed closely by the Broadway-Hale takeover of Stockton department store Smith and Lang Company. The old Smith and Lang was renamed Weinstock, Lubin, sending the Sacramento brand outside its home territory for the first time since the short-lived 1898 San Francisco store. The new store being built at Weberstown was scheduled to open in the fall of 1965, just in time for the holiday shopping season. On the day the Weberstown opening schedule was announced, Broadway-Hale Stores shares were listed on the New York Stock Exchange.[18]

Changes were underway in Sacramento, as well. Marion Armstrong retired as Weinstock, Lubin's president shortly after the department store's ninetieth-anniversary celebration. A few months later, Weinstock, Lubin's new president, Norman Wechsler, and Hale's president, Bill Ahern, announced the merger of operations of both companies. Although the department stores had run competing businesses in physical proximity to each other for decades, no plans were made to close or consolidate stores in spite of consolidating office operations. Instead, Hale's continued to operate at Arden Fair and at its Ninth and K Street location just three blocks from Weinstock, Lubin. For its part, Weinstock, Lubin continued to operate its Twelfth and K flagship store, Country Club Plaza and the two new stores in Stockton. Hale's also continued operating under that brand in San Francisco and San Jose. The merged operations were headquartered at the Twelfth and K Street Weinstock, Lubin store. To the customer, the greatest change was the new single monthly statement that replaced separate bills from each department store. For Broadway-Hale, the merger firmly established the chain as the dominant department store operation in the Sacramento area. *Time* magazine named the twenty-eight-store Broadway-Hale chain the West's largest department store group, with a $30-million-a-year operation and 1964 sales reaching a record $219 million.[19]

Things had reached a point of confusion in the Sacramento market, however. Now there were department stores in the region noted variously as Weinstock's, Hale's, Weinstock, Lubin and Weinstock-Hale. The

The Arden Fair Hale's became Weinstock's in 1967 in conjunction with an overall name change that standardized all Weinstock, Lubin and Hale's properties in Sacramento as simply Weinstock's.

announcement of a new store breaking ground at the Florin Center shopping complex was followed closely by the announcement of a store closure in another city and a name change for Sacramento: the Hale's on Mission Street in San Francisco would close because it was "not compatible" with the remainder of the company's operation, and all Weinstock-Hale properties would be known simply as "Weinstock's." Now, Broadway-Hale was operating two Weinstock's within three blocks of each other, at Ninth and K and Twelfth and K. Despite persistent rumors to the contrary, there were no plans to close either K Street location.[20] The odd placement of two Weinstock's on K Street would remain for the next three years.

Approaching the First One Hundred Years

In the ensuing years, Broadway-Hale continued to expand and add greater depth to its retail offerings. In 1967, Weinstock's opened its first department store outside California, in Reno's Park Lane Shopping Center. Shortly thereafter, Broadway-Hale announced a merger with Neiman-Marcus Co. of Dallas. Under the terms of the merger, Neiman Marcus became a division of Broadway-Hale, similar to the structure in place for Weinstock's. Approaching its 100th anniversary, Weinstock's was now part of a huge retail chain that included Broadway department stores in Southern California, Arizona and Nevada; Weinstock's in Sacramento, Stockton, Fresno and Reno; Emporium-Capwell—in which Broadway-Hale held a majority interest—in the San Francisco Bay Area; and Neiman-Marcus. The Fresno Weinstock's, which opened on September 1, 1970, was the eighth store bearing the Weinstock's name.[21]

The growth of Weinstock's continued at a fairly aggressive pace. A new store opened on Sunrise Boulevard in Citrus Heights on Valentine's Day 1972. The store was designed from the inside out in what was called a "cubistic" concept, with the departments designed first and the store itself designed around the departments. The cubistic design created by the Charles Luckman Associates architectural firm was intended to express the "many individual shops which make up the larger department store."[22]

When the Sunrise store opened, it was mobbed.

At 10:00 a.m., when the ribbon was cut by Miss Sacramento Linda Jonason, the parking lot was packed, and hundreds of people rushed into the new store for the special opening sale. Highway patrol officers had to be dispatched to the roof of the store to help direct traffic; among the civic representatives attending the opening were Sacramento mayor Richard

The 1972 opening of Weinstock's on Sunrise Boulevard in Citrus Heights showed a shift in architecture. Called a "cubistic" concept, the store was designed from the inside out, and the design was intended to express the individual shops that make up the department store.

Marriott, Sacramento county supervisor Eugene T. Gualco and state assemblyman Walter W. Powers. As the Sunrise store opened, a new power structure was put in place that reflected Broadway-Hale's growth and the value of the ever-expanding company. In a sweeping series of management changes, Prentis C. Hale became chairman of a new executive committee of the board of directors, Edward W. Carter was named chairman of the board and Philip M. Hawley was named president of the parent company.[23]

The structure for Carter Hawley Hale was now in place.

VI
FROM CENTENNIAL CELEBRATION
TO TAKEOVER TARGET,
1974-1995

*Under this roof your interests are protected. Were you the merchant and
we the guest, we feel sure there would be no change in the principles and
practices of this house.*
—David Lubin

A reporter writing about the 100th anniversary of Weinstock's posed the question, "After 100 years as one of the most successful retail outlets in the nation, what do you do for an encore?" The response from Broadway-Hale president Philip M. Hawley was simple and to the point: "Look forward to the next 100 years." Indeed, in 1974 there was no reason to believe the next one hundred years would not be as dynamic as the first. Under the umbrella of Broadway-Hale Stores, Weinstock's continued to approach merchandising with an eye toward innovation. In addition, Broadway-Hale was about to finalize a name change that further reflected the impressive record of its key executives, Edward Carter and Philip Hawley, to become Carter Hawley Hale Stores. But for Sacramento employees, Weinstock's still retained a "family company" feel, due in large part to Broadway-Hale corporate policy. According to Philip Hawley, local people were given total autonomy and wide latitude to make decisions.[1]

The 1974 100th-anniversary celebration of Weinstock's brought together current and former company executives, including former president Marion Armstrong (center) and Philip M. Hawley (right), president of Carter Hawley Hale.

JUST A LITTLE CONSOLIDATION AMID EXPANSION

In 1967, when Broadway-Hale announced that the company would use only the Weinstock's name in Sacramento and that it would change all department stores bearing the names Weinstock, Lubin, Hale's and Weinstock-Hale to fall in line with the official nomenclature, rumors and speculation began about the fate of one or both of the stores at Ninth and K and Twelfth and K Streets. These rumors continued into the mid-1970s as locals and industry-watchers pondered the efficacy of keeping two downtown stores within three blocks of each other while the company targeted all of its other expansion at spreading the brand into the suburbs, throughout the Central Valley and into other western states.

In the context of weakening business activity on K Street, executives considered other uses for the property. At one point, there was speculation in the press that the Ninth and K Weinstock's would be leased to the state for office space. A downtown Sacramento construction suspension during Ronald Reagan's tenure as governor had left a shortage of space for the growing number of state employees. City officials, led by Sacramento mayor Phillip Isenberg, pushed to locate more state workers to vacant downtown buildings as a means of reversing the decline of downtown business. Ultimately, executives sold Weinstock's at Ninth and K to Kimmel Properties, which planned to reposition the site as a mixed-use commercial and office space. Some of the employees had worked at the store for thirty or more years, beginning their careers when the location was Hale's and Weinstock's was their main competitor. With the closure of the Ninth and K store, the employees went to the other five Weinstock's stores in Sacramento. For some, that meant moving three blocks up K Street to Twelfth and the company's flagship store. For others, it meant adjusting to the newer stores, such as Florin and Sunrise. "I've been here so long," said Helen Campbell, who worked in the cosmetics department. "I've seen mothers get pregnant, have babies, seen the babies grow up and come back to me to buy cosmetics. And I can also remember when old-timers would bring me pickles and jam from home."[2]

Once the Ninth and K Street store was closed, executives announced their plans for the flagship store at Twelfth and K.

With Sacramento's downtown economy in decline, city officials viewed the announcement that Weinstock's planned to exercise its option on the old location of historic Sacramento furniture store Breuners on the K Street Mall near Sixth Street as a big step in the process of downtown revitalization. The plan called for closing the Twelfth and K location once the new site was ready for occupation. Mayor Phillip Isenberg released a statement saying the decision by Weinstock's was the culmination of many months of cooperation between the City of Sacramento, the Housing and Redevelopment Agency, Downtown Plaza Properties and Carter Hawley Hale.[3]

Detailed project plans unveiled in 1977 revealed that the new 205,000-square-foot store would be three stories and house not only a modern department store but also Weinstock's headquarters. The store would be built over subterranean parking for 480 cars. Most striking among the new design's features was a series of Romanesque arches at the K Street and L Street entrances. Carter Hawley Hale's decision to build an entirely new store at this location was viewed as evidence of executives' faith in Sacramento. It was, as a company press release noted, the sixth time in Weinstock's 103-year history that plans were announced for another new Sacramento downtown store. "Now," the press release noted, "Weinstock's will be returning close to its original home with a new store located at Sixth Street between the K Street Mall and L Street, on property which for years was the home of another historic Sacramento-based retailer, The John Breuner Company."[4] Of course, the press release did not remark that the original Fourth and K Street site was now home to rival Macy's.

The new flagship store took two years to complete. The contemporary design of the store conveyed both the stability of the firm's more than one hundred years in the community and Carter Hawley Hale's belief in the long-range economic viability of Sacramento. Carter Hawley Hale regarded Sacramento as an important market. Studies conducted by the company brought changes to merchandising strategy reflected in the new downtown flagship store. One study indicated that fully half of Weinstock's adult female market was now composed of "career women" who had a need to shop quickly and, in many cases, were less price-sensitive than executives had previously thought. To that end, a "designer's department" was added

Glass arches created a striking entrance for the new downtown store at Sixth and K Streets. The opening of the new flagship store in 1979 was seen as evidence of Carter Hawley Hale's confidence in Sacramento.

to the new downtown store plan. With this concept, a professional woman—pressed for time and less concerned with price—would be able to arrange an appointment with a designer, who would help her choose her wardrobe. The styles available in Weinstock's were very forward-looking for their time. As one buyer for women's better sportswear noted, Neiman Marcus, as part of Carter Hawley Hale, was so "cutting-edge" that it had a lot to say about the overall trends and direction for Weinstock's.[5] In other words, women in Sacramento were benefitting from the "fashion sense" of a Weinstock's/Neiman Marcus association.

The unveiling of the Downtown Plaza store was quite an event. Touted as the new flagship store, executives made deliberate ties between the Sixth and K site and the original store, and reminders of the company's 105-year history in downtown Sacramento were seen everywhere. Those who attended the benefit preview the night before the store's official opening entered through a plank-floored, brick-tiled area called the Pavilion—perhaps a nod to the temporary site that housed the department store after

Unidentified store executives are seen here examining the historic photographs on a wall at Harris & David's, an in-store restaurant designed to invoke Weinstock, Lubin's past. Circa 1979.

the 1903 fire. A restaurant in this section, called Harris and David's, directly invoked the spirit of the founders and featured photos of the half brothers and scenes from their company history as part of the décor. Features in the restaurant deliberately pointed to the fact that the new store was as close as possible to the site of the original ten- by twelve-foot one-price mercantile established by David Lubin in 1874.[6] Carter Hawley Hale made a point of using the store's history to keep it firmly tied to the community.

Sadly, the closing of the Twelfth and K Street store did not receive the respect it warranted. Recall that in 1924, when the store opened, U.S. representative Grove Johnson ceremoniously locked the doors at Fourth and K for the final time the night before Simon Lubin opened the doors at the Twelfth and K Street location. But in 1979, a little more than a half century later, the sole focus on the closure of the beautiful Twelfth and K store seemed to be the final bargains snatched up by shoppers and the extra care that was being taken to guard against shoplifting. One young Twelfth and K employee noted, paradoxically, that she was "glad [the old store's] gone," but she would miss it because it had "more character than the new store."[7]

Philip Hawley at the press party and opening gala for the new downtown flagship store in November 1979. He is being interviewed by KCRA Channel 3 reporter Mike Boyd.

"A Consumer Is a Statistical Abstract. A Customer Is a Person."

Flagship store location aside, one thing that had not changed at Weinstock's throughout its long history was the strong commitment to customer service, a commitment executives deliberately intensified into the mid-1980s. This was by no means a philosophy among department stores nationwide. Some in the retail industry stated that many shoppers, in particular those too young to have shopped prior to World War II, had not been exposed to good customer service and, in some cases, might not care about such a thing. The Weinstock's assumption, however, was that customer service provided value. It was even considered one of Philip Hawley's measures of a successful retailer. In addition to growth in sales volume, he said, success was also measured by "the store's stature in the community, the professionalism of its management, the extent to which it is people-sensitive with both customers and employees, and how well it responds to change."[8]

Weinstock's had always been both an innovator and an employee-centric organization and did not change under Carter Hawley Hale. Janey Shugart, whose career at Weinstock's took her to the level of buyer, recalled that Weinstock's invested heavily in its employees. It was, she noted, a wonderful place to start a career because the company not only trained you but also put financial and emotional thought into its employees to the degree that you knew the company was incredibly invested in you. Shugart experienced firsthand the kind of innovation for which David Lubin and Harris Weinstock had been known. When she started with the company in 1979, everything was still tracked manually. "You wouldn't get results from sales until the end of the week," she said. Retailers were just beginning to transition to computers, and Weinstock's was at the forefront. During the transition, staff was sent to weeklong learning sessions for training. "All of a sudden everything's becoming computerized," she said of the period, "and you can track what is selling and who's selling it, and you're able to monitor your stock so much more closely."[9]

Shugart took Weinstock's early adaptation of computer technology a step further in her role as a buyer for women's better sportswear. She won a Carter Hawley Hale contest for writing a productive program for the store's computer system. Her prize? A portable IBM computer. At this time, "portable" meant a computer weighing sixty pounds but still luggable from place to place. Shugart hauled her new computer to New York on a buying trip, and one of her stops was Liz Claiborne. As she tells it, Claiborne was so "hot" that the priority status on shipping orders was based on when buyers got their orders in. Shugart spent a few days at the Claiborne studio viewing the line and then a few nights at her portable computer, working with her program.

> *It would give me my Modesto store versus my Sunrise store versus my Utah store…You know you're 5 percent of sales, this is 10 percent…And I could take the group and dissect it as to what items [to order]. By the time I left New York, I usually could be leaving [Liz Claiborne] an order, which was unheard of because that could take you a week or two. You'd probably go home from market and spend a great deal of time doing it manually and fine-tuning it. It was just a really cool thing to be with Carter Hawley Hale, who was on the forefront of computerized selling, and then to be involved with Liz Claiborne, who was the designer in the 1980s, and get this computer to kind of pull everything together with support from the company.*[10]

In the fall of 1980, Weinstock's grew to twelve stores with the opening of two new Weinstock's in Utah—one in Salt Lake City and the other in Ogden. Carter Hawley Hale was now considered one of the leading retail operations in the country. In addition to Weinstock's and Neiman Marcus, its other department store divisions included: thirty-nine Broadway stores in Southern California; the Broadway Southwest, with nine stores in Arizona, Nevada and New Mexico; six Capwell's stores in Oakland and San Francisco; twelve Emporium stores in San Francisco, Santa Rosa, San Jose and along the peninsula; twenty-six Thalhimer's stores in southern Virginia and North Carolina; and sixteen John Wanamaker's in the Greater Philadelphia area. The company's other subsidiaries included Waldenbooks, national mail-order firm Sunset House and Contempo Casuals.[11]

A "FEISTY SITUATION"

By the early 1980s, Carter Hawley Hale had experienced tremendous growth by acquiring more and more companies; some industry watchers believed that the Los Angeles–based retailing conglomerate had acquired more companies than it had demonstrated an ability to handle. Suddenly, in 1984, the tables were turned. An "upstart" Ohio retailer launched an aggressive bid for Carter Hawley Hale.[12]

The Limited was a fashion specialty retailer that had recently acquired the Lane Bryant chain, the retail chain Roaman's and the California lingerie chain Victoria's Secret. Analysts widely considered The Limited to be one of retailing's best-managed chains, and its founder and chairman, Leslie H. Wexner, went after Carter Hawley Hale with guns blazing. Financial and retail analysts described the takeover bid as "one of those feisty situations pitting unlikely, but intriguingly similar, executives against one another."[13] This was shaping up to be a showdown between Leslie Wexner and Philip Hawley.

In its initial offer, The Limited sought 53.6 percent of Carter Hawley Hale's common stock—20.3 million shares—at $30 per share. Remaining shareholders would be able to exchange one share of Carter Hawley Hale for 1.32 common shares of The Limited. The combined offer—a stock purchase in excess of $600 million and a stock swap valued at $500 million—was $1.1 billion, the retail sector's biggest takeover bid to date. A source close to Carter Hawley Hale characterized the takeover bid as "the minnow trying to swallow the whale." By the time The Limited announced its bid, it had purchased some 700,000 shares of Carter Hawley Hale. The announcement sent Carter Hawley Hale shares to a nine-year high. "Wexner thinks that he can conquer the world," one analyst reportedly said, but "Phil Hawley has enough ego, too, to turn around and make a merger on his own just to block Wexner."[14]

Indeed, it appeared that Carter Hawley Hale had lined up enough bank credit lines to enable Hawley to attempt to either purchase its shares on the open market or to tender an offer for shares of The Limited. Other analysts speculated that Carter Hawley Hale might sell off one of its "crown jewels"—Neiman Marcus or Waldenbooks—or some of

Philip M. Hawley, president of Carter Hawley Hale, grew the company by acquiring other businesses, making Carter Hawley Hale one of the leading retail operations in the country. Things changed when he was forced to fight off two takeover attempts by Leslie H. Wexner, founder and chairman of The Limited. Circa 1974.

its California holdings in order to raise money to defend itself against The Limited's takeover attempt. At the same time, Carter Hawley Hale sued The Limited in an effort to stop the takeover attempt, charging the upstart with violating securities laws and failing to disclose potential antitrust problems.[15]

Wexner replied by ramping up the pressure. The Limited filed a statement with the Securities and Exchange Commission that stated the company would solicit written consent from Carter Hawley Hale's shareholders to remove Carter Hawley's board of directors. The company also requested authorization for a special Carter Hawley Hale shareholders meeting for the sole purpose of replacing the board. Silent up to this point, Carter Hawley Hale announced that its board would not be deterred from carefully evaluating all of the available alternatives before responding to the tender offer. Within the retail industry, however, there was a growing perception that Carter Hawley was moving too slowly in responding to the offer. As a result, uncertainty grew within Carter Hawley Hale's divisions, damaging morale. Both executives and employees expressed concern over their jobs. Rather than respond to The Limited's offer, however, Carter Hawley announced that it had raised $900 million in lines of credit with a group of banks. At the same time, Carter Hawley's board adopted a bylaw that, in effect, eliminated the possibility of The Limited dismissing the board even if it were able to acquire 51 percent of the stock. But the announcement only served to fuel Wall Street speculation that Carter Hawley planned to acquire another retailer—a move that would make it more costly for The Limited to succeed in its takeover bid. A new acquisition could also raise antitrust issues with federal officials.[16]

Carter Hawley's next move came from somewhere out of left field. The retail giant sold one million shares of new convertible preferred stock to the General Cinema Corporation—the country's largest film exhibitor— for $300 million in cash. The deal gave General Cinema a 22 percent share of Carter Hawley's common stock, on a diluted basis, making it the single biggest shareholder of the company. In addition, General Cinema was represented on Carter Hawley Hale's board and acquired a six-month option to purchase the Waldenbooks chain for about $285 million. The Limited sought an injunction to block the plan, but a federal judge in Los Angeles denied the request. Nevertheless, the New York Stock Exchange (NYSE) raised concerns of its own. Did the sale of stock to General Cinema constitute a transfer of control of the company, and if so, did it violate Exchange rules? According to NYSE rules, shareholders had to vote before 18.5 percent of a company could be transferred to one investor.[17]

With Carter Hawley Hale buying its own stock, The Limited contemplated increasing its cash offer for Carter Hawley Hale common stock from thirty dollars per share to thirty-five dollars per share. Carter Hawley Hale directors convened a special Saturday session and unanimously rejected The Limited's offer, stating that the revised tender offer was "inadequate." Among the board's cited concerns: "a takeover under the new terms would create a debt load so large that The Limited would be forced to sell some key Carter Hawley divisions." Following on the heels of this announcement, however, the Securities and Exchange Commission (SEC) charged Carter Hawley Hale Stores with violating securities law by buying more than 50 percent of its outstanding shares on the secondary market—which, in its view, amounted to a tender offer—and therefore had to proceed through certain steps not taken by Carter Hawley Hale. The SEC called on Carter Hawley to rectify the situation by declaring a stock dividend that would restore the common shares outstanding to the level that had prevailed before the company made its stock purchase.[18]

Philip Hawley responded in confident "bring it on" fashion. "We welcome the opportunity to have the issue presented to the courts." Leslie Wexner made sure his voice was heard as well: "I believe that what we have here is a business Watergate. Carter Hawley's management is pushing a lot of laws and rules of moral judgment. It has serious New York Stock Exchange, SEC and Labor Department problems. If we are wrong and the SEC is wrong, I think that the public company is dead." Others waded into the fray, as well. One investment banker who asked to remain anonymous said the situation was "so complex that a massive and comprehensive settlement will have to be made and that the developments will last from seven to eight months, with major changes in both concerns." A federal judge now issued a temporary restraining order against Carter Hawley Hale, prohibiting it from purchasing any more of its stock. Yet, following a review, U.S. District Court judge A. Wallace Tashima rejected the SEC's injunction and allowed Carter Hawley to proceed with its strategy against The Limited's hostile takeover bid. In an amended filing with the SEC, The Limited charged that the stock repurchase program by Carter Hawley Hale violated California law. The Limited then extended its thirty-five-dollars-per-share tender.[19]

How much of the wrangling was personal? One reporter noted that "retailing's biggest takeover battle appears, first of all, to be a fight for Mr. Hawley to save face. The 58-year-old executive is defending his company, the nation's sixth-largest retailing chain, against The Limited, a smaller specialty chain based in Columbus, Ohio, that the 46-year-old Mr. Wexner has built up." On May 21, The Limited ended its tender offer but vowed to carry on a court challenge over Carter Hawley's tactics. In its fight against The Limited's hostile takeover attempt, Carter Hawley Hale ultimately bought 17.9 million shares of its own stock and issued $300 million in preferred stock to General Cinema Corporation, which now owned a one-third voting control over Carter Hawley Hale.[20]

The Limited, whose takeover bid resulted in its ownership of 698,805 shares of Carter Hawley, announced it would solicit proxies in an effort to elect two of its nominees to the Carter Hawley board at the upcoming annual meeting. Carter Hawley responded by delaying the meeting "to allow time for the processing of proxy materials"; in other words, time to mount a defense against The Limited's bid for seats on the board. Because The Limited was attempting to use California's cumulative voting law—which allowed shareholders to use one vote for each position or allocate all those votes for one or two positions—to its advantage, Carter Hawley launched an effort to change its state of incorporation from California to Delaware, where cumulative voting was not required. The Limited filed suit to prevent the change, but on review, a judge allowed the change in the state of incorporation, noting that the proposed move was a legal way for the corporation to protect itself. Shortly thereafter, The Limited dropped its efforts to elect two directors to the board of Carter Hawley Hale.[21]

Yet the six-week battle cost Carter Hawley Hale dearly. To pay for the stock repurchases, the corporation sold its profitable Waldenbooks division to the Kmart Corporation. Moreover, the deal with General Cinema left the latter with seven people on the Carter board and in a position to reap substantial annual dividends from the convertible preferred stock that Carter Hawley Hale had issued. The company's modernization efforts covering 270 stores also proved costly. Soft profit margins, however, were beginning to improve, and things were looking up.[22]

Not to be deterred, The Limited began preparing for another run at the retail giant.

More Takeover Attempts, Restructuring and Layoffs

This time, The Limited came in with a partner. Ohio shopping mall magnate Edward J. DeBartolo Sr. formed a partnership with Wexner and The Limited for the sole purpose of acquiring Carter Hawley Hale. This time, the offer was fifty-five dollars per share, twenty dollars higher than the final share price offered two years ago. Carter Hawley rejected it, and in doing so, it announced that it would split off its specialty store business—Neiman Marcus, Bergdorf Goodman and Contempo Casuals—into a separate, publicly owned chain called the Neiman-Marcus Group. Under the plan, Carter Hawley Hale would continue with two Broadway Stores divisions, Emporium Capwell, Thalhimers and Weinstock's—the second most profitable division of Carter Hawley Hale. In 1987, as the restructuring was taking place, the department stores had only recently begun showing improvement through a renewed emphasis on customer service. Philip Hawley still believed very strongly in the value of a department store's position in the community and familiarity among its customers. The history of the Weinstock's brand in Sacramento was one of the department store's most important assets.[23]

Many in the industry wondered about the spinoff strategy. More and more, analysts viewed department stores as "mature"; specialty stores were the "new wave" of retailing. But Carter Hawley believed that department stores were undergoing a revival. Philip Hawley was banking on the idea that department stores like Weinstock's held nearly institutional status in their communities and that the department store format was gaining in retailing. He also hedged his bet by instituting cost-cutting programs and production changes to improve efficiency. Other changes that he sought to implement included more store modernization and an expansion of private label business. Weinstock's stores, beginning with the Florin Mall location, were slated for a three-year, $25 million face-lift. The Arden Fair store remodeling coincided with the construction of Sacramento's first Nordstrom department store, a retailer Carter Hawley characterized as "complementary" to Weinstock's.[24]

Yet things did not improve as Carter Hawley Hale expected. The recession and the Persian Gulf War had hit the retailing industry hard. In addition, Carter Hawley carried a huge debt load incurred fighting off the second takeover attempt by The Limited and DeBartolo. Two 1990 buyout offers for the Weinstock's division by Fresno-based chain Gottschalks were turned down. Reportedly, Carter Hawley asked about buying the Fresno chain but received no response. Retail analysts questioned Carter Hawley's dismissal of the Gottschalks offer, noting that selling off individual divisions might be the quickest way to improve the company balance sheet, now weighed down with long-term debt amounting to about $1.5 billion. One analyst noted that selling off Weinstock's made the most sense because it had a "real live buyer." Within one week of the news of the rebuffed buyout,

Weinstock's announced it would eliminate about one thousand jobs over the next twelve to eighteen months. At the same time, Carter Hawley sold off East Coast division Thalhimers to the May Company. The pressure was now off to sell any other divisions, including Weinstock's, but the elimination of jobs was a blow. A Carter Hawley spokesman noted that the one thousand planned job cuts amounted to about 3 percent of its 36,500-member workforce. But this was not to be the end; additional job cuts came with the new year, including a small number at Weinstock's, and Carter Hawley Hale eliminated the Sacramento department store's commission-based pay structure. Originally initiated as one means of building excellent customer service, the commission-based pay structure fell victim to the desperate need for Carter Hawley to improve its ailing balance sheet.[25]

THE LAST OF THE OLD-LINE MERCHANTS

Within two weeks of the announced layoffs, Carter Hawley Hale took another hit. Two national bond-rating agencies slashed their ratings for the retail giant. Standard and Poor's and Moody's Investment Service downgraded Carter Hawley Hale, a move widely seen as advance notice of either a major restructuring or a Chapter 11 bankruptcy filing. Suppliers now became reluctant to ship goods to Carter Haley Hale stores, including Weinstock's. The headline in the *Sacramento Union* newspaper less than one week later said it all: "Carter Hawley Hale Is Broke."[26]

On Monday, February 11, 1991, Carter Hawley Hale Stores sought bankruptcy protection by filing Chapter 11 and stopped paying interest on its bonds, which had plummeted to junk status. The company sought bankruptcy protection because it was unable to secure bank and trade credit financing and not because its brands were suffering. A number of analysts felt that it had a good chance of emerging from bankruptcy as a leaner, stronger company, as other large retailers had done.[27]

Weinstock's employees shared analysts' optimism. "At least we know where we stand," said one employee, echoing the sentiments of many. Delores Seymour, an employee at the Arden Fair store, was much more specific: "My theory is Chrysler Corp did it and look at them now. I think we may have some Lee Iacocca types," she noted, referring to the Chrysler CEO credited with turning around that corporation. Some analysts, however, were skeptical that creditors would allow the company to survive intact and predicted the sale of some or all of Carter Hawley's eighty-eight stores. Rather than a store sell-off, however, Carter Hawley consolidated administrative, merchandising and support staff among the twenty-two-store Emporium chain and the twelve-store Weinstock's chain. The result was the loss of almost all Weinstock's headquarters jobs. But although operations were consolidated, store identities remained distinct.[28]

Carter Hawley Hale was not alone in the Chapter 11 arena; a number of department store companies were in the same retail dilemma. Indeed, R.H. Macy and Co. filed for Chapter 11 bankruptcy protection less than one year after Carter Hawley's filing, and Federated Department Stores had emerged from bankruptcy and was poised to become a larger company with national chain aspirations.[29]

Carter Hawley outlined a reorganization plan in July 1992 that a federal bankruptcy judge approved. Carter Hawley Hale would emerge from bankruptcy protection by the end of September 1992, nineteen months after the filing date. Philip Hawley was optimistic: "This reorganization plan is designed to enable Carter Hawley Hale to move forward on a financially sound basis so that it can compete vigorously in its markets." Carter Hawley's largest secured creditors, The Prudential and Bank of America, supported the plan. Seventy-five percent of the ownership of the company would devolve to the Zell-Chilmark Fund, a company set up by Chicago businessman Sam Zell, who had purchased most of Carter Hawley's unsecured debts. Zell, a longtime acquaintance of Hawley, had bailed out other distressed companies. Philip Hawley noted that the plan would allow the company to concentrate 100 percent on the business, not the bankruptcy. Creditors and shareholders approved it. But as one reporter wrote, "The question now is whether the reorganized retailer can achieve its aims of upgrading aging stores, broadening its customer base and stocking more fashionable goods in light of the worst economic downturn in California since the Great Depression."[30]

The day after Carter Hawley Hale Stores emerged from Chapter 11 bankruptcy, Philip Hawley announced his retirement.

Comments came swiftly and included noting "the true passing of an era" on one end to "From hindsight, he [Philip Hawley] made one of the colossal errors of the 1980s. Although his name is still up in lights, it's a much dimmer bulb," on the other end. Perhaps one of the finest, most generous comments about the man himself came from *New York Times* reporter Andrea Adelson: "Mr. Hawley is one of the last of the old-line merchants who started his career on the shop floor and ended with his name on the door."[31] Adelson's comment represented what would be missed in the changing face of retailing—the chief executive who had actually worked on the shop floor.

The reorganized company moved forward with a new name: Broadway Stores. Within two months of the resignations of both CEO Philip Hawley and Carter Hawley Hale president H. Michael Hecht, the three Weinstock's locations in Utah began liquidation sales in preparation for store closures.[32]

By the summer of 1995, new bankruptcy fears had taken hold at Broadway Stores. Several credit companies refused to guarantee payment to the company's suppliers and Standard & Poor's placed the Broadway Stores' $144 million in debt on credit watch. Broadway Stores announced that it was exploring financing alternatives and that the company had been in talks with the May Department Stores Company to sell the Emporium and Weinstock's stores. That deal, however, fell through, as Broadway Stores agreed to merge with Federated Department Stores. Ohio-based Federated operated 354 department stores, including Macy's, Bloomingdale's, Bullock's, Bon Marche, Stern's and Lazarus. Industry analysts said that Broadway Stores had little choice but to allow itself to be acquired. What Philip Hawley had fought so hard against in 1984 and 1986 ultimately happened anyway. For many in Sacramento, it meant the end of an era. Almost as soon as the merger with Federated was announced, the company stated that it did not intend to keep the Weinstock's name; the stores would be renamed, sold off or closed. This was neither unexpected nor unusual under the circumstances. But as *Sacramento Bee* writer Mark Glover noted, many residents believed that when Weinstock's went, a part of Sacramento's soul would go with it.[33]

Perhaps that is a bit heavy-handed. If Weinstock's were truly a valued part of Sacramento's "soul," why were fewer people shopping there? As the general manager of Arden Fair Mall noted, when it was announced that the Arden Fair Weinstock's would become a Macy's, "Macy's will be a stronger draw for the center than Weinstock's." And a local retail analyst said that while the prospect of losing about 150 local jobs from the Florin Mall store slated for closure was sobering, those employees would at least have some benefits packages and opportunities within Federated. Federated, he noted, was keeping a lot of stores and converting them to Macy's, not "just closing stores and chopping jobs wholesale." Weinstock's, like many "home grown" department stores, had been steadily losing market share owing to changes in shopping habits. The inability to finance store modernization and keep constantly changing, fashionable merchandise in front of customers caused the parent company—and by extension Weinstock's—to fall behind the competition. Trying to revamp perception and catch up to stores that had seized market share like Nordstrom, Macy's, The Limited and The Gap proved ultimately fruitless.[34]

After 122 years, "Sacramento's finest department store" was gone.

Conclusion
"GOODBYE, WEINSTOCK'S"

And while Weinstock's has not been locally owned for some 65 years,
Weinstock's—perhaps because of the name and its history—often seemed
more like a local business than the outlet of a national chain.
—Sacramento Bee

Department store mergers, buy-outs and consolidations were not
unusual during the 1990s. But Weinstock's—even after it became part
of the Broadway-Hale/Carter Hawley Hale chain—had maintained its
local character and its place in the community, and that's why the end hurt
so much for so many people. It was the loss of a beloved institution, and its
past was part of our own. As one regular Weinstock's customer put it, "The
thought that there will be no more stores called Weinstocks in Sacramento
is kind of sad. I remember my great-grandmother talking about shopping
at Weinstock's."[1]

Interestingly, similar sentiments about the store's role in family's lives can
be found in letters dating back to the early 1900s. The letters were sent to
Weinstock, Lubin & Co. and remained in the corporate files:

> *How well I remember when in my real youthful days I would come from*
> *Chico with my grandparents on a visit to Sacramento and these special*
> *occasions were always accompanied with a shopping list and inevitably to*
> *my great pleasure and delight our path led straight to Weinstock, Lubin and*
> *Company, then at Fourth and K Streets.*

I worked for Weinstock, Lubin & Co. in 1918 and during my employment there bought most of [the] *articles for my "Hope Chest."*

We are old timers here as we remember the old Mechanics Store…We the Porter family of Roseville district all join hands in wishing you many more happy, prosperous birthdays.[2]

A November 21, 1995 editorial in the *Sacramento Bee* noted the sense of loss. The name had been a Sacramento landmark for well over one hundred years, and it had been a major factor in the city's life. It was difficult to imagine the Weinstock name disappearing even though local ownership had ended long ago. The store often seemed more like a local business than the outlet of a national chain. At its core, that's what it was—what it had always been—a local business. Even though it was rumored at the time that Federated might convert the downtown Weinstock's into a Bloomingdale's, the promise of an upscale retailer—a possibility that never came close to fruition—could not blunt the concern over the store's changeover:[3]

[The] *decision* [by Federated] *to convert Weinstocks will hardly be an unmixed blessing. It means scores of employees will be laid off and many more will face an uncertain future. It also means that a name that's been a Sacramento landmark for nearly 120 years—and a major factor in the city's life—will be gone from the local scene.*[4]

A sense of loss over the passing of a local landmark—like today's interest in the history of department stores such as Weinstock's—speaks to the power of place and the personal meaning of public spaces. Weinstock's and other businesses like it were more than just department stores; they were places where people gathered. As such, they were an integral part of the life of the community.

I believe that Philip Hawley wanted to maintain the Weinstock's brand. Had the economy been different in the wake of the hostile takeover attempts, he might have succeeded. Unfortunately, when Philip Hawley left a reorganized Carter Hawley Hale, the last of the venerable department store's protections left with him.

Well, perhaps not all protections left with Philip Hawley. As the story goes, a longtime Weinstock's employee working in the office at the Sixth and K Street store realized that there were boxes of old business records, photographs, employee newsletters and other Weinstock's memorabilia in danger of being tossed out as the chain of stores converted to Macy's. At her request, the material was gathered up and donated to the Center for Sacramento History, the archive for the city and county of Sacramento, where it was cataloged, preserved and is available for scholarly research. For her part in preserving the history of Weinstock, Lubin & Co., Sacramento owes a debt of gratitude.

NOTES

CHAPTER I

1. Olivia Rossetti Agresti, *David Lubin: A Study in Practical Idealism* (Boston: Little, Brown and Company, 1922), 41–42; *Living a Principle through Half a Century*, Weinstock, Lubin & Co. fiftieth anniversary booklet, William & Shirley Gaylord Collection, Center for Sacramento History; *Sacramento Bee*, "Weinstock-Lubin History Is Told," February 18, 1916; Reva Clar and William M. Kramer, "Chinese-Jewish Relations in the Far West: 1850–1950, Part II," *Western States Jewish History* 21 (1989): 141–42.
2. Agresti, *David Lubin*, 14–16.
3. Ibid., 16–17.
4. Ibid., 19–25; Harris Weinstock, "Tribute to David Lubin," *Weinstock, Lubin & Co. Store Bulletin* 4, no. 1 (January 1919), Weinstock-Lubin Collection, Center for Sacramento History.
5. Agresti, *David Lubin*, 22–24. The story of Lubin's forced departure from his brother Simon was recounted by Lubin in a 1910 letter to his son, Jesse.
6. Agresti, *David Lubin*, 26–32.
7. Ibid., 19–25, 30–33; Weinstock, "Tribute."
8. Agresti, *David Lubin*, 33–37.
9. Ibid., 38–39.
10. Ibid., 39; William Leach, *Land of Desire: Merchants, Power and the Rise of a New American Culture* (New York: Vintage Books, 1994), 123; Juliann

Sivulka, *Soap, Sex and Cigarettes: A Cultural History of American Advertising* (Belmont, CA: Wadsworth Publishing Company, 1998), 46–51.

11. Agresti, *David Lubin*, 39–40; Henry C. Klassen, "T.C. Power & Bro.: The Rise of a Small Western Department Store, 1870–1902," *Business History Review* 66, no. 4 (Winter 1992): 675; "A Bit of History as Told by Mr. David Lubin," Weinstock, Lubin & Co., Leaflet No. 3, April 22, 1916, Weinstock-Lubin Collection, Center for Sacramento History.

12. Agresti, *David Lubin*, 40–41; *Living a Principle*. While this story is recounted in many places, most of this version, complete with the direct quotes, comes from Lubin's friend and biographer Olivia Rossetti Agresti.

13. "A Bit of History"; Willard Thompson, "David Lubin's Vision: Why a Sacramento Pioneer Got a Street and a Library in Rome Named for Him," *Sacramento Bee*, March 23, 1986; Agresti, *David Lubin*, 40, 46.

14. Jan Whitaker, *Service and Style: How the American Department Store Fashioned the Middle Class* (New York: St. Martin's Press, 2006), 138.

15. *Sacramento Daily Bee*, 1875–1877.

16. Klassen, "T.C. Power & Bro.," 674; Vicki Howard, "'The Biggest Small-Town Store in America': Independent Retailers and the Rise of Consumer Culture," *Enterprise & Society* 9, no. 3 (September 2008): 467.

17. *Weinstock & Lubin Fall and Winter 1881–82 Illustrated Catalogue and Song Book*, Weinstock-Lubin Collection, Center for Sacramento History.

18. Ibid.; Whitaker, *Service and Style*, 54.

19. Regina Lee Blaszczyk, *Imagining Consumers: Design and Innovation from Wedgwood to Corning* (Baltimore, MD: Johns Hopkins University Press, 2000), 65; Leach, *Land of Desire*, 23.

20. *Illustrated Catalogue and Song Book*; Mary Praetzellis and Adrian Praetzellis, *The Mary Collins Assemblage: Mass Marketing and the Archaeology of a Sacramento Family* (Rohnert Park, CA: Anthropological Studies Center, Sonoma State University, 1990), 22–23; Pamela Walker Laird, *Advertising Progress: American Business and the Rise of Consumer Marketing* (Baltimore, MD: Johns Hopkins University Press, 1998), 28–29; *Weinstock, Lubin & Co. Spring and Summer 1891* (1891; repr., Sacramento American Revolution Bicentennial Committee, 1975).

21. Steven M. Avella, *Sacramento: Indomitable City* (Charleston, SC: Arcadia Publishing, 2003), 72–73; "His Brother's Partner," Weinstock's Centennial Album, *Sacramento Union*, March 17, 1974; Board of Directors Minutes, January 31, 1888–November 8, 1896, Weinstock-Lubin Collection, Center for Sacramento History.

22. *Sacramento Observer*, "Weinstock's Celebrates 100 Exciting Years in Merchandising," March 21–27, 1974.

23. Leach, *Land of Desire*, 20; *Spring and Summer 1891*; *Sacramento Daily Bee*, "A Splendid Structure: Completion of Sacramento's Mammoth Mercantile House," November 28, 1891; *Sacramento Daily Bee*, November 24, 1891.

24. William R. Leach, "Transformations in a Culture of Consumption: Women and Department Stores, 1890–1925," *Journal of American History* 17, no. 2 (September 1984): 322–26.

25. Leach, *Land of Desire*, 55–56; Whitaker, *Service and Style*, 133.

26. Leach, *Land of Desire*, 57–61; Leach, "Transformations in a Culture of Consumption," 325; Whitaker, *Service and Style*, 109.

27. *Sacramento Daily Bee*, "A Splendid Structure: Completion of Sacramento's Mammoth Mercantile House," November 28, 1891; Avella, *Indomitable City*, 65–66.

28. *Sacramento Union*, "Memories of Days Gone By," Weinstock's Centennial Album, March 17, 1974.

CHAPTER II

1. Agresti, *David Lubin*, 77–79; Jerry Hagstrom, "David Lubin Established Foundation for What Would Become FAO," *Agweek*, July 11, 2011, http://www.agweek.com/event/article/id/18741 (accessed September 14, 2011); "A Man with Vision," Weinstock's Centennial Album, *Sacramento Union*, March 17, 1974.

2. Lubin patent numbers, including patent 357152 for the Lubin clod crusher and cultivator, as well as eight additional agriculture-related patents, UC Berkeley Bancroft Library, the Magnes Collection, Manuscript Collections, BANC MSS Magnes Collection on David Lubin; "A Man with Vision."

3. Avella, *Indomitable City*, 75–76; "His Brother's Partner"; Agresti, *David Lubin*, 97–102, 111–21.

4. H.G. Wells, *The World of William Clissold: A Novel at a New Angle*, vol. 2 (New York: George H. Doran Company, 1926), 582–83; "His Brother's Partner."

5. Susan Porter Benson, *Counter Cultures: Saleswomen, Managers and Customers in American Department Stores, 1890–1940* (Urbana: University of Illinois Press, 1986), 15; Leach, "Transformations in a Culture of Consumption," 327.

6. Board of Directors Minutes, January 31, 1888–November 8, 1896; Weinstock's Centennial Album, *Sacramento Union*, March 17, 1974; Whitaker, *Service and Style*, 89; "First Annual Report of the Co-operative

Association of the Employees of Weinstock, Lubin & Co., 1907–1908, William & Shirley Gaylord Collection, Center for Sacramento History.

7. *San Francisco Call*, "Lubin Seeks a Divorce," May 10, 1896; *Sacramento Bee*, "Lubin-Steinman," May 11, 1896.

8. Ibid.; UC Berkeley Bancroft Library, Magnes Collection, Manuscript Collections, BANC MSS Magnes Collection on David Lubin.

9. *Sacramento Bee*, "Lubin-Steinman."

10. *San Francisco Call*, "Lubin Seeks a Divorce"; *Sacramento Bee*, "Lubin-Steinman."

11. *Sacramento Bee*, "Lubin-Steinman."

12. Ibid.

13. Agresti, *David Lubin*, 131–36.

14. Ibid., 138–44.

15. Letter by Harris Weinstock, August 26, 1903, placed in the cornerstone of the 1904 building, Weinstock-Lubin Collection, Center for Sacramento History; Agresti, *David Lubin*, 148–54.

16. Letter by Harris Weinstock, August 26, 1903; *75 Years of Service to Sacramento*, William & Shirley Gaylord Collection, Center for Sacramento History.

17. "The Fire of a Year Ago, and the Changes It Brought," January 1904, Weinstock-Lubin Collection, Center for Sacramento History; Whitaker, *Service and Style*, 96–97.

18. *Sacramento Bee*, "Weinstock & Lubin's Great Store Falls a Wholesale Prey to the Flames," January 31, 1903.

19. Ibid.

20. Ibid.

21. *75 Years of Service*; *Living a Principle*; Letter by Harris Weinstock, August 26, 1903; *Sacramento Record-Union*, "Pluck and Indomitable Will Are Still Factors in the Firm," February 2, 1903.

22. Letter by Harris Weinstock, August 26, 1903.

23. Whitaker, *Service and Style*, 96–97; "Weinstock & Lubin's Great Store Falls."

24. Letter by Harris Weinstock, August 26, 1903.

25. "The Fire of a Year Ago"; *Living a Principle*.

26. Letter by Harris Weinstock, August 26, 1903; "Expectations of the Future," Weinstocks Centennial Album, *Sacramento Union*, March 17, 1974.

CHAPTER III

1. Harris Weinstock, a tribute to David Lubin, *Weinstock, Lubin & Co. Store Bulletin*, vol. 4, no. 1, January, 1919, Weinstock-Lubin Collection, Center for Sacramento History; Willard Thompson, "David Lubin's vision," *Sacramento Bee*, March 23, 1986; and Agresti, 120-130, 165-168.

2. Hagstrom, "David Lubin Established Foundation"; Weinstock, "Tribute to David Lubin"; Thompson, "David Lubin's Vision"; Agresti, *David Lubin*, 165–82.

3. Weinstock, "Tribute to David Lubin"; Thompson, "David Lubin's Vision"; Agresti, *David Lubin*, 197–202.

4. Wells, *World of William Clissold*, 583–85.

5. Steven M. Avella, *The Good Life: Sacramento's Consumer Culture* (Charleston, SC: Arcadia Publishing, 2008), 124–15; "His Brother's Partner."

6. "Wives and Daughters," Weinstocks Centennial Album, *Sacramento Union*, March 17, 1974; "His Brother's Partner"; *Sacramento Bee*, "Weinstock, Writer, Takes His Own Life," March 3, 1936.

7. *Sacramento Bee*, "Simon J. Lubin Dies in Hospital in San Francisco," April 15, 1936.

8. *Sacramento Bee*, Weinstock, Lubin & Co. advertisements, February 25, 1911; February 27, 1911.

9. *Sacramento Union*, "Memories of Days Gone By."

10. *Sacramento Bee*, "Harry Thorp, Capitalist, Dies in Hospital," September 14, 1920; Report to the Stockholders of Weinstock, Lubin & Co., February 14, 1912, Weinstock-Lubin Collection, Center for Sacramento History; Gayle Gullett, "Women Progressives and the Politics of Americanization in California, 1915–1920," *Pacific Historical Review* 64, no. 1 (February 1995): 77; Meg Jacobs, *Pocketbook Politics: Economic Citizenship in Twentieth-Century America* (Princeton, NJ: Princeton University Press, 2005), 48–49.

11. Report to the Stockholders of Weinstock, Lubin & Co., February 14, 1912, Weinstock-Lubin Collection, Center for Sacramento History.

12. *Sacramento Bee*, "Senators Consult David Lubin on Rural Credits Legislation," July 25, 1914; Agresti, *David Lubin*, 301, 324–25.

13. Agresti, *David Lubin*, 326–27.

14. *Sacramento Bee*, "Lubin to Talk on National Defenses," February 14, 1916; Agresti, *David Lubin*, 327.

15. *Sacramento Bee*, "Local Firm Gives $3,034 to Red Cross," May 16, 1917; "Store Bulletin: Weinstock, Lubin & Co.," August 1, 1918, Weinstock-Lubin Collection, Center for Sacramento History.

16. Avella, *The Good Life*, 125.

17. *Sacramento Bee*, "Weinstock, Lubin Plans Skyscraper," November 9, 1917.

18. Ibid.; Richard Longstreth, *The American Department Store Transformed, 1920–1960* (New Haven, CT: Yale University Press, 2010), 83.

19. *Sacramento Bee*, "Site for Million Dollar Store is Changed to J St.," September 3, 1919; *Sacramento Bee*, "Reorganization for Weinstock-Lubin Co.," July 1, 1919; *Sacramento Bee*, "Board of Managers Chosen for Weinstock-Lubin Co.," August 2, 1919; "The New Organization: Weinstock, Lubin & Co., Sacramento, California," Weinstock-Lubin Collection, Center for Sacramento History.

20. *Sacramento Bee*, "Activity Is Brisk on Upper J Street," November 15, 1919; Ruth Annette Kassis, "A Buzz in the Ether: The Sacramento Bee, Radio and the Public Interest, 1922–1950" (master's thesis, California State University, Sacramento, 2010), 58.

21. *Sacramento Bee*, "Plans Completed for Big Department Store," December 31, 1919.

22. Agresti, *David Lubin*, 345–48.

23. Recollection of Dorothy Sophie Lubin Heller, March 20, 1975, UC Berkeley Bancroft Library, Magnes Collection, Manuscript Collections, BANC MSS Magnes Collection on David Lubin; *Sacramento Bee*, "David Lubin Dies at Rome," January 2, 1919; *Sacramento Bee*, "David Lubin Leaves $600,000 Estate to Widow and Children," April 2, 1919; David Lubin, *Let There Be Light: The Story of a Workingmen's Club, Its search for the Causes of Poverty and Social Inequality, Its Discussions, and Its Plans for the Amelioration of Existing Evils* (New York: G.P. Putnam's Sons, 1900), 43.

24. *Sacramento Bee*, "Impressive Service for David Lubin," March 7, 1919; Agresti, *David Lubin*, 349.

25. Jacobs, *Pocketbook Politics*, 53; Whitaker, *Service and Style*, 38, 198, 256.

26. *Sacramento Bee*, November 11–4, 1919.

Chapter IV

1. *Sacramento Bee*, "Department Store Sells Property on K Street," April 9, 1920; *Sacramento Bee*, "Wrecking Crew is Paving Way for $1,000,000 Store," April 19, 1920.

2. *Sacramento Bee*, "Weinstock, Lubin Site Is Ready for Excavation," May 22, 1920; *Sacramento Bee*, "Plans for Building Big Store Halted," May 24, 1920.

3. *Sacramento Bee*, "Plans for Building Big Store Halted," May 24, 1920; Robert A. Divine et al., *The American Story*, 3rd ed. (New York: Pearson Longman, 2007), 656.

4. *Sacramento Bee*, "L Street Store for Weinstock, Lubin Rumored," November 16, 1921; *Sacramento Bee*, "Weinstock, Lubin Building Traded in $800,000 Deal," July 20, 1922.

5. Kassis, "A Buzz in the Ether," 62.

6. Ibid.; *Sacramento Bee*, "An Apology," Weinstock, Lubin & Co. advertisement, December 13, 1920.

7. Kassis, "A Buzz in the Ether," 62; *Sacramento Bee*, "Weinstock-Lubin Offers to Conduct the Bee," December 13, 1920.

8. Weinstock, Lubin & Co. advertisement, *Sacramento Bee*, *Sacramento Union* and *Sacramento Star*, December 14, 1920.

9. *Sacramento Union*, "Sale of Lynching Bee Postals Stopped; Fox Waxes Wrathy," December 15, 1920.

10. Benson, *Counter Cultures*, 109; Whitaker, *Service and Style*, 275.

11. "Weinstock, Lubin Home to be at Twelfth and K," *Sacramento Bee*, April 21, 1923.

12. Steven M. Avella, *Sacramento and the Catholic Church: Shaping a Capital City* (Reno: University of Nevada Press, 2008), 155–58; *Sacramento Bee*, "Weinstock, Lubin Home to Be at Twelfth and K," April 21, 1923; *Sacramento Bee*, "Weinstock-Lubin Work Begins About June 1st," May 5, 1923.

13. Longstreth, *American Department Store*, 13; Bradford Kimball & Co. to Simon J. Lubin, June 28, 1923, Weinstock-Lubin Collection, Center for Sacramento History.

14. Longstreth, *American Department Store*, 23; *Sacramento Bee*, "Weinstock, Lubin Store in New Shopping Center," October 11, 1923; *Sacramento Bee*, "Building Permits Reflect Steady Growth of City," April 12, 1924; Weinstock, Lubin & Co. scrapbook, Weinstock-Lubin Collection, Center for Sacramento History; "The Modern Store Building, the Subject of Talk by C.H. Hails," *Cooperator* 4, no. 9 (October 30, 1923), Weinstock-Lubin Collection, Center for Sacramento History; *Sacramento Bee*, "Weinstock, Lubin Firm Sets Date to Occupy New Store," May 3, 1924.

15. *Sacramento Bee*, "Weinstock, Lubin Firm Sets Date to Occupy New Store," May 3, 1924; *Store News* 500, no. 139, Weinstock-Lubin Collection, Center for Sacramento History.

16. *Sacramento Bee*, Weinstock, Lubin & Co. open house advertisement, June 2, 1924; *Sacramento Bee*, "Large Crowd Attends Opening Reception of

Weinstock-Lubin Store," June 2, 1924; *Store News* 500, no. 140, Weinstock-Lubin Collection, Center for Sacramento History; "Echoes of Fifty Years," Weinstock-Lubin Collection, Center for Sacramento History.

17. *Sacramento Union*, "How Times Have Changed," March 17, 1974; *Living a Principle*.

18. *Living a Principle*.

19. *Sacramento Union*, "Memories of Days Gone By" and "How Times Have Changed."

20. *Sacramento Bee*, "Weinstock, Lubin Files Articles," February 5, 1926; *Sacramento Bee*, "New Capital Is Secured by Big Sacramento Firm," March 3, 1926.

21. Avella, *The Good Life*, 125–26; *Sacramento Bee*, "Department Stores Help Make City Retail Shopping Hub," July 2, 1927; *Sacramento Bee*, "Department Stores Boom City as Retail Shopping Center," October 12, 1929.

22. Longstreth, *American Department Store*, 33; Whitaker, *Service and Style*, 20.

23. *Sacramento Bee*, "Lubin Resigns in Midst of Ouster Talk," November 23, 1934; *Sacramento Bee*, "Lubin Dies in Hospital"; *Sacramento Bee*, "Lawrence Ellis Back from Buying Trip Is Optimistic for Future," February 5, 1932.

24. *Sacramento Bee*, "59th Birthday of Weinstock, Lubin Is Feted," October 6, 1933; Jacobs, *Pocketbook Politics*, 109.

25. *Sacramento Bee*, "Weinstock-Lubin Notes are Bought," March 16, 1934; *Sacramento Bee*, "Lubin Resigns."

26. *Sacramento Bee*, "Weinstock Lubin Store Is to be Razed," October 29, 1934; *Sacramento Bee*, "Cornerstone Box Yields Prophecy of City's Growth," June 22, 1935; Letter by Harris Weinstock, August 26, 1903.

27. *Sacramento Bee*, "Lubin Dies in Hospital"; unknown newspaper, "Carmel Man Takes Own Life," circa 1957, Mary G. Heller Cope Collection (unprocessed), Center for Sacramento History.

28. *Sacramento Bee*, "Two Stores Pay Cash Bonuses to Employees," November 21, 1936.

29. *Sacramento Bee*, Weinstock, Lubin & Co. advertisement and radio broadcasting program listings, July 23, 1937; *Sacramento Bee*, Weinstock, Lubin & Co. advertisement, April 26, 1937; *Sacramento Bee*, "Window Gazers Are Entertained by Magic Light," April 27, 1937.

30. *75 Years of Service*.

31. Memos from Wallace McBain, December 10, 1941; December 19, 1941, Weinstock-Lubin Collection, Center for Sacramento History; Avella, *Indomitable City*, 107–08.

32. Letter from N.C. Smith, Wilmore Steamship Company to Laura Lubin Saqui, February 16, 1944, Mary G. Heller Cope Collection (unprocessed), Center for Sacramento History; *San Francisco Chronicle*, "Lubin's Rome Farm Institute Left Untouched by Fascists," July 8, 1944.

CHAPTER V

1. *Sacramento Facts 1953: The Land the Lord Remembered* (Sacramento, CA: Sacramento Chamber of Commerce, 1953), 7–11.
2. Lizabeth Cohen, "From Town Center to Shopping Center: The Reconfiguration of Community Marketplaces in Postwar America," in *The Gender and Consumer Culture Reader*, edited by Jennifer Scanlon (New York: New York University Press, 2000), 245–47; Avella, *The Good Life*, 135.
3. Whitaker, *Service and Style*, 24, 141, 214.
4. *Sacramento Bee*, "Weinstock, Lubin Leases Property for Expansion," September 6, 1945; *Sacramento Bee*, "Youth Center Store Will Open Oct. 25th," October 17, 1946.
5. *Sacramento Bee*, "Youth Center Store"; Nancy Phillips, *A Place of Our Own: Childhood Recollections of Weinstock's Department Store*, edited by James C. Scott, November 25, 2009, DVD, Sacramento Public Library, Sacramento Digital Stories series.
6. *Sacramento Bee*, "Store's New Electric Stairways Are in Use," September 24, 1947; Whitaker, *Service and Style*, 93.
7. Memo to the employees of Weinstock-Lubin, circa August 1949, Weinstock-Lubin Collection, Center for Sacramento History.
8. *Sacramento Bee*, "Weinstock-Lubin Will Enlarge Mezzanine," April 17, 1950; *Sacramento Bee*, "Expansion Work in Department Store Has Begun," May 27, 1950.
9. "Mrs. Marion Armstrong Named W-L President," *Co-Operator* 2, no. 2 (May 26, 1951), Weinstock-Lubin Collection, Center for Sacramento History; Whitaker, *Service and Style*, 186–87.
10. *Sacramento Bee*, "Weinstock-Lubin Will Open Parking Lot by Fall," March 6, 1953; *Sacramento Bee*, Weinstock-Lubin & Co. advertisement, March 15, 1952; *Sacramento Bee*, "Weinstock-Lubin Parking Space Will Be Expanded," July 9, 1954; and Whitaker, *Service and Style*, 27.
11. *Sacramento Bee*, "Weinstock-Lubin Wins Window Display Awards," March 13, 1952; *Sacramento Bee*, "Weinstock-Lubin Wins Award for Ad in Bee," January 4, 1955; *Sacramento Bee*, "KFBK AM and FM Tune in Time,"

September 2, 1953; Gloria Glyer, "Good Old Days" documentary footage, KVIE Collection, Center for Sacramento History; KVIE, "Importance of Baseball in Sacramento in the 1930s," http://video.answers.com/importance-of-baseball-in-sacramento-in-the-1930s-304058072 (accessed December 9, 2011).

12. Cohen, "From Town Center to Shopping Center," 247; Avella, *Indomitable City*, 127–28; Longstreth, *American Department Store*, 233–36.

13. Cohen, "From Town Center to Shopping Center," 247; Avella, *Indomitable City*, 127–28; Longstreth, *American Department Store*, 234.

14. "History of the A.G. Kassis Enterprise," unpublished memoir of Frank Kassis, October 25, 1982, private collection.

15. Ibid.; *Sacramento Bee*, "$6 Million W-L Store Is Set for Suburbs," April 16, 1959; *Sacramento Bee*, "New W-L Store Will Open March 4th," January 20, 1961; "The New Arden Fair Hale's," Weinstock-Lubin Collection, Center for Sacramento History.

16. *Sacramento Bee*, "10,000 Are Invited to Weinstock Store Opening," February 16, 1961; *Sacramento Bee*, "$7 Million W-L Store Is Open to Public," March 4, 1961; *Sacramento Bee*, "W-L Preview Will Start at 7 PM," March 3, 1961; *Sacramento Bee*, "Preview of W-L Raised $4,000 for Hospitals," March 4, 1961.

17. Cohen, "From Town Center to Shopping Center," 253.

18. *Sacramento Bee*, "Stockton Store Will Bear Weinstock-Lubin Name," April 5, 1962; *Sacramento Bee*, "Weinstock Will Take Over Stockton Store," January 15, 1963; *Sacramento Bee*, "Weinstock, Lubin Plans Store on Stockton Mall," May 11, 1964; *Sacramento Bee*, "Broadway-Hale Stock Goes on NY Exchange," May 11, 1964.

19. *Sacramento Bee*, "Weinstock, Hale's Will Join Operations," August 18, 1965; *Time*, "Department Stores: The West's Biggest Chain," September 24, 1965, http://www.time.com/time/magazine/article/0,9171,834385,00.html (accessed July 6, 2011).

20. *Sacramento Bee*, "Ground Breaking for Weinstock-Hale's Signals Start on $22-Million Center," June 27, 1966; *Sacramento Bee*, "Weinstock-Hale Firm Closes Store in SF," February 16, 1967; Douglas Dempster, "Just Plain Weinstock's: Department Store Will Change Name," *Sacramento Bee*, May 16, 1967.

21. *Sacramento Bee*, "Weinstock Expansion," August 6, 1967; *Sacramento Union*, "Neiman-Marcus, Hale Agree to Merge," October 24, 1968; "Weinstock's 'Gift Box' Store," *Stores: The Retail Management Magazine* (October 1970): 14, 34.

22 "Weinstock's New Look: Sunrise Store Will Be Divided Into Cubes," *Sacramento Bee*, March 28, 1971; and "Pioneer of Sunrise Center Ready for That First Day," *Sacramento Union*, February 13, 1972.

23. John Burns, "Sunrise Ave. Weinstock's Opens," *Sacramento Bee*, February 14, 1972; *Sacramento Union*, "Weinstock's Opening Mobbed," February 15, 1972; *Sacramento Bee*, "Broadway-Hale Names Hart Lyon to LA Post," February 25, 1972.

Chapter VI

1. *Sacramento Union*, "Weinstock's Marks Start Here in 1874," March 14, 1974; *Sacramento Observer*, "Weinstock's Celebrates 100 Exciting Years in Merchandising," March 21–27, 1974.
2. Doug Dempster, "State Building Thaw: 9th, K Weinstock's to Be Office?" *Sacramento Bee*, December 18, 1975; *Sacramento Bee*, "Office Building Future For 9th, K Weinstock's," July 27, 1976; Mel Assagai, "Weinstock's 9th And K Departure Sad One for Older Hands," *Sacramento Bee*, October 17, 1976.
3. Steve Gibson, "Weinstock's Plans Downtown Store," *Sacramento Bee*, March 12, 1977.
4. *Sacramento Bee*, "Weinstock's Unveils Plans for 3-Story Store on K Street Mall," October 29, 1977; Weinstock's Downtown Plaza Press Release, Fall 1979, Weinstock-Lubin Collection, Center for Sacramento History.
5. Weinstock's Downtown Plaza Press Release, Fall 1979; *Sacramento Union*, "New Weinstock's to Open Nov. 3," September 21, 1979; Janey Shugart, interview by author, June 30, 2011.
6. "A Flagship Store Nears Unveiling," *Sacramento Bee*, October 14, 1979; John Burns, "Nostalgic Touch," *Sacramento Bee*, October 26, 1979; "Weinstock's opening nears," *Sacramento Union*, November 1, 1979; and Jean Towell, "A Preview Of The New Weinstock's," *Sacramento Bee*, November 1, 1979.
7. *Sacramento Bee*, "12th and K Store Closes: Shoppers Bid Weinstock's Adieu," November 2, 1979.
8. Marguaret Peterson, "Weinstock's Pioneered Service Effort: Local Chain Leapfrogs Other Stores," *Sacramento Bee*, November 18, 1985; Weinstock's new employee brochure, circa 1979, private collection of Janey Shugart.
9. Janey Shugart, interview by author, June 30, 2011.
10. Ibid.
11. Draft of Weinstock's History and Parent Corporation, Weinstock-Lubin Collection, Center for Sacramento History.
12. Isadore Barmash, "Carter Hawley Girds for Fight," *New York Times*, April 9, 1984.

13. Isadore Barmash, "Carter Hawley Silent on Offer," *New York Times*, April 4, 1984.

14. Isadore Barmash, "Carter Hawley Bid by Limited," *New York Times*, April 3, 1984; Barmash, "Silent on Offer."

15. *New York Times*, "Carter Hawley," April 6, 1984; *New York Times*, "Carter Hawley's Advice on Offer," April 7, 1984; Barmash, "Girds for Fight."

16. Isadore Barmash, "Limited Steps Up Pressure," *New York Times*, April 11, 1984; Isadore Barmash, "Carter's $900 Million Credit," *New York Times*, April 13, 1984.

17. Isadore Barmash, "Carter Acts to Foil Bid by Limited," *New York Times*, April 17, 1984; *New York Times*, "Court Backs Carter Hawley," April 18, 1984; Raymond Bonner, "Carter Sale of Stock Is Queried," *New York Times*, April 19, 1984.

18. Isadore Barmash, "Limited May Raise Carter Hawley Bid," *New York Times*, April 25, 1984; *New York Times*, "Limited's Bid Rejected," April 30, 1984; Isadore Barmash, "Carter Gain Seen in Bid for Stock," *New York Times*, May 1, 1984; Isadore Barmash, "Carter Faces Suit by S.E.C.," *New York Times*, May 2, 1984; Isadore Barmash, "S.E.C. Sues Carter on Stock Actions," *New York Times*, May 3, 1984.

19. Isadore Barmash, "S.E.C. Case Welcomed by Carter," *New York Times*, May 4, 1984; *New York Times*, "Judge Bars Carter from Buying Stock," May 5, 1984; *New York Times*, "S.E.C. Loses Bid to Thwart Carter," May 9, 1984; *New York Times*, "Limited Assails Carter Move," May 15, 1984; *New York Times*, "Bid for Carter Extended Again," May 16, 1984.

20. Thomas C. Hayes, "The Embattled Chief of Carter Hawley Defends His Moves," *New York Times*, May 7, 1984; *New York Times*, "Limited Ends Bid for Carter," May 22, 1984.

21. *New York Times*, "Limited Seeking Seats at Carter," May 30, 1984; *New York Times*, "Carter Hawley to Delay Meeting," June 8, 1984; *New York Times*, "Carter Defense," June 15, 1984; *New York Times*, "Limited Files Suit," June 29, 1984; *New York Times*, "Carter Hawley Reincorporation," July 13, 1984; *New York Times*, "Limited Drops Carter Tactic," July 17, 1984.

22. Nicholas D. Kristof, "The Carter Hawley Hale Solution," *New York Times*, November 14, 1985.

23. Larry Hicks, "$1.8 Billion Bid for Carter Hawley," *Sacramento Bee*, November 26, 1986; *New York Times*, "Carter Hawley Silent on Offer," December 1, 1986; Isadore Barmash, "Higher Bid Ended After Carter Rebuff," *New York Times*, December 9, 1986; Larry Hicks, "Weinstock's

Parent OKs Restructuring," *Sacramento Bee*, August 27, 1987; Larry Hicks, "Retailer's 'Divorce': Weinstock's Parent Splits Itself in Two," *Sacramento Bee*, September 28, 1987.

24. Larry Hicks, "Carter Hawley Stirs from Slumber," *Sacramento Bee*, November 21, 1988; Martha J. Alcott, "Weinstock Stores to Get Face-Lift," *Sacramento Bee*, November 23, 1988.

25. Martha J. Alcott, "Weinstock's Rebuffs Buyout Offer," *Sacramento Bee*, October 5, 1990; Martha J. Alcott, "Retailer Plans Job Cutbacks—Weinstock's to Be Affected by Paring," *Sacramento Bee*, October 11, 1990; Martha J. Alcott, "Weinstock's Cuts Staff, Changes Pay Structure," *Sacramento Bee*, January 26, 1991.

26. Martha J. Alcott, "Bond Woes Hit Weinstock's Owner," *Sacramento Bee*, February 6, 1991; E. Scott Reckard, "Carter Hawley Hale Is Broke," *Sacramento Union*, February 12, 1991.

27. Reckard, "Carter Hawley Hale Is Broke"; Marguaret Peterson, "Odds Good for Exiting Chapter 11," *Sacramento Bee*, February 12, 1991.

28. Martha J. Alcott, "Weinstock's Parent Firm Seeks Chapter 11 Protection," *Sacramento Bee*, February 12, 1991; Richard W. Stevenson, "Chapter 11 for Carter Hawley," *New York Times*, February 12, 1991; Isadore Barmash, "Carter Hawley Is Said to Plan Consolidation," *New York Times*, April 20, 1991.

29. Mark Glover, "Plaza Sees ailing Anchor Stores as Gems," *Sacramento Bee*, February 11, 1992.

30. *New York Times*, "Carter Hawley Gives Debt Plan," July 8, 1992; Mark Glover, "Carter Hawley Reorganization OK'd," *Sacramento Bee*, July 30, 1992; *New York Times*, "Bankruptcy Judge Backs Carter Hawley Hale," July 30, 1992; Mark Glover, "Reorganization Could Benefit Shareholders," *Sacramento Bee*, July 31, 1992; *New York Times*, "Carter Hawley Reorganization Plan Approved by Judge," September 15, 1992; Andrea Adelson, "Backed by Zell Investment, Carter Hawley Re-emerges," *New York Times*, October 9, 1992.

31. Andrea Adelson, "Retirement Set at Carter Hawley Hale," *New York Times*, October 10, 1992; George White, "Carter Hawley Chief to Retire," *Los Angeles Times*, October 10, 1992.

32. *New York Times*, "President of Carter Hawley Hale Resigns," November 4, 1992; *Deseret News*, "Weinstocks Stores Start Liquidation Sale," December 2, 1992; Max B. Knudson, "Shoppers Saying 'Good Buy' to 3 Utah Weinstocks Stores," *Deseret News*, December 20, 1992.

33. *New York Times*, "Bankruptcy Fears Take Big Toll on Broadway Stores' Shares," August 8, 1995; Cathleen Ferraro and Norman D. Williams,

"Weinstock's Parent Finds White Knight," *Sacramento Bee*, August 15, 1995; Mark Glover, "Sale of Weinstock's Means End of Era," *Sacramento Bee*, August 20, 1995.

34. Mark Glover, "Three Weinstock's to Become Macy's," *Sacramento Bee*, November 18, 1995; Martha J. Alcott, "Weinstock's Parent Firm Seeks Chapter 11 Protection," *Sacramento Bee*, February 12, 1991.

Conclusion

1. Mark Glover, "Historic Name on Way Out," *Sacramento Bee*, August 16, 1995.
2. Mrs. A.W. Fouts to S.J. Lubin, October 11, 1926; Mrs. J.C. Purcell to S.J. Lubin, October 15, 1926; Mrs. Robert Porter to Weinstock, Lubin & Co., October 22, 1926, Weinstock-Lubin Collection, Center for Sacramento History.
3. *Sacramento Bee*, "Goodbye, Weinstock's," November 21, 1995.
4. Ibid.

ABOUT THE AUTHOR

Annette Kassis studied journalism at Louisiana State University, Shreveport, and history at California State University, Sacramento, and the University of California, Santa Barbara. Her primary areas of research are media, advertising, mass consumption and consumerism and popular culture, with a particular interest in the history of media in Sacramento and the western United States. Formerly a co-owner of the Sacramento-based advertising agency K&H Marketing, LLC, she continues to work in communications and public relations in California. To learn more, visit www.kassishistorical.com or follow her on Twitter @AnnetteKassis.

Visit us at
www.historypress.net